STO

ACPL

3 1833 038

P9-BVG-586

DISCARDED

NOV 2 2 2000

Ruthless Trust

Also by Brennan Manning

Reflections for Ragamuffins

The Boy Who Cried Abba

Abba's Child

The Signature of Jesus

The Ragamuffin Gospel

Lion and Lamb

A Stranger to Self-Hatred

Souvenirs of Solitude

The Wisdom of Accepted Tenderness

The Gentle Revolutionaries

Prophets and Lovers

Ruthless Trust

The Ragamuffin's Path to God

BRENNAN MANNING

HarperSanFrancisco
A Division of HarperCollins*Publishers*

All biblical quotations are from The Jerusalem Bible unless otherwise indicated (Doubleday and Company, New York, 1966).

RUTHLESS TRUST: *The Ragamuffin's Path to God.* Copyright © 2000 by Brennan Manning. All rights reserved. Printed in the United States of America. No part of this book may be used or reproduced in any manner whatsoever without written permission except in the case of brief quotations embodied in critical articles and reviews. For information address HarperCollins Publishers, Inc., 10 East 53rd Street, New York, NY 10022.

HarperCollins books may be purchased for educational, business, or sales promotional use. For information please write: Special Markets Department, HarperCollins Publishers, Inc., 10 East 53rd Street, New York, NY 10022.
HarperCollins Web site: http://www.harpercollins.com
HarperCollins®, ®, and HarperSanFrancisco™ are trademarks of HarperCollins Publishers, Inc.

FIRST EDITION

Book design by Helene Wald Berinsky

Library of Congress Cataloging-in-Publiscation Data

Manning, Brennan
Ruthless trust : the ragamuffin's path to God / Brennan Manning.
1st ed.
p. cm.
Includes bibliographical references.
ISBN 0-06-251709-0 (cloth)
1. Trust in God—Christianity. 2. Christian Life. gl. Title

BV4637 .M314 2000
241'.4—dc21 00-059717

00 01 02 03 04 ❖RRD(H) 10 9 8 7 6 5 4 3 2 1

To

Jesus of Nazareth,

who so longed for our trust that

he died for love of it

CONTENTS

FOREWORD

WHEN OUR CHILDREN were young I would sometimes rise early on a Saturday morning and fix them pancakes for breakfast. It was all great fun—the broken eggs, the spilt milk, the batter and the chatter. They loved pancakes—even my pancakes—and they would wolf them down quickly. I would often watch in astonishment at their greedy eating. Not once did I see either of them slipping a few pancakes under the table, stuffing them in their pockets thinking, "I don't know about Dad. Maybe there won't be any pancakes tomorrow and so I'd better get myself a little stash just in case." Not once did they ask me about the price of eggs or my ability to secure enough milk for tomorrow. No, as far as they were concerned there was an endless supply of pancakes. They lived, you see, in trust.

Trust is in short supply in our day. I have seen, for example, many a church with the word "faith" in its name: Faith Bible Chapel, Faith Community Church, Faith Ministries International. But I have yet to find a church with the word "trust" in the name. Trust, I say, is in short supply. It is for this reason that I welcome the perceptive thoughts of Brennan Manning on this often neglected but vital subject.

Manning ties the word "ruthless" to the word "trust"—*Ruthless Trust*. It is a juxtaposition that at first glance startles us, for ruthlessness refers to action that is "without pity." But it is right here that we catch our first glimpse into Manning's ingenious approach to this topic, for by calling us to "ruthless trust" he is really standing against all the "self-pity" that plagues modern culture. He is calling us to a trust that stoutly refuses to regard self-interest as the highest good in life. This book, in fact, is a frontal attack on all the egocentric, hyphenated self-sins of our day: self-indulgence, self-will, self-service, self-aggrandizement, self-gratification, self-righteousness, self-sufficiency, and the like.

Manning calls this decisive movement into a radical trust in God "a second conversion." And it is indeed. Conversion involves *both* a turning toward and a turning away. In our turning toward God we are learning to turn away from "the world, the flesh and the Devil." We are also turning away from ourselves as the be-all and end-all of life, for we are slowly but surely realizing that God is truly the heart and center of all things.

I am so glad that Manning does not slide over the

tragedies of our human existence easily in his eagerness to call us to a living trust in God. He is willing to face head-on the gnawing question we all feel deep inside: "How does one dare to propose the way of trust in the face of raw, undifferentiated heartache, cosmic disorder and the terror of history?" He even admits that these heart-wrenching realities of life often become "the trust-busting anguish of many struggling seekers." Manning seeks not only to raise the question of the grim reality of evil but also to provide an answer—to the extent that finite human beings can have an answer.

Now, I must not give away Manning's answer here: that I will leave for you to discover for yourself as you read and think and pray. But I will give you one hint. Look for his answer not so much in the didactic teaching as in the stories he tells. And Brennan Manning is a master story-teller. (As an aside, I very much like the way he is able to move effortlessly from stories of past centuries to stories of our day as if they comprise a seamless robe—and so they do!) But be forewarned, Manning tells stories in the ancient way of wisdom teaching so that the answer is not predigested and obvious. No, you must search for yourself. His stories, like all good stories, require prayerful thought and reflection.

Ruthless Trust brings a timely message for our day. Even more, it calls us to a life that is for all time and eternity.

RICHARD J. FOSTER

PREFACE

ALWAYS AND EVERYWHERE the overriding issue for the ragamuffin rabble is the person of Jesus Christ.

Who and what are the ragamuffins? The unsung assembly of saved sinners who are little in their own sight, conscious of their brokenness and powerlessness before God, and who cast themselves on his Mercy. Startled by the extravagant love of God, they do not require success, fame, wealth, or power to validate their worth. Their spirit transcends all distinctions between the powerful and powerless, educated and illiterate, billionaires and bag ladies, high-tech geeks and low-tech nerds, males and females, the circus and the sanctuary.

"Here is a saying that you can rely on and nobody should doubt, 'that Christ Jesus came into the world to save sinners' (1 Tim. 1:15). Unglued and undone by personal experience of the Messiah of sinners, who searches the noisy streets of large cities and the unpaved roads of small hamlets, the ragamuffin walks the way of ruthless trust in the irreversible forgiveness of the Master. The defenses he has erected against his own truth as a saved sinner wither in the maelstrom of mercy flashing like lightning across his life.

"If the Lord Jesus Christ has washed me in his own blood and forgiven all my sins," the ragamuffin whispers to herself, "I cannot and must not refuse to forgive myself."

The ragamuffin resonates to the Pauline cry, "I *know* who it is that I have put my trust in" (2 Tim. 1:12). The *felt* knowledge of the tenderness of Jesus that lifts us, scarred and depressed after sin, gently to himself is the very soul of ragamuffin spirituality. After stumbling and falling, the ragamuffin does not sink into despondency and endless self-recrimination; she quickly repents, offers the broken moment to the Lord, and renews her trust in the Messiah of sinners. She knows that Jesus is comfortable with broken people who remember how to love.

Alert to the manipulations and machinations of pharisaical self-righteousness, ragamuffins refuse to surrender control of their lives to rules and regulations. They see that the stale religiosity of legalists, trapped in the fatal narcissism of spiritual perfectionism, obscures the face of the God of Jesus. They will not barter their souls for the false security of fear-filled pieties that cripple the human spirit. The motto on the New Hampshire license plate, "Live free or die," is the ragamuffin motto.

During the past three years of prayer, study, and soul-searching, the Holy Spirit has guided me to an inescapable conclusion: ruthless trust is *the* way for *this* ragamuffin. If it be your way, the sign you can trust will be the slow, steady, and miraculous transformation from self-rejection to self-acceptance rooted in the acceptance of Jesus Christ.

BRENNAN MANNING
New Orleans
15 March 2000

ACKNOWLEDGMENTS

THE ENTHUSIASTIC ENCOURAGEMENT of Kathy Helmers at Alive Communications in Colorado Springs and Stephen Hanselman at HarperSanFrancisco provided the motivation to finish this book. Kathy was also instrumental in my writing of chapter three, "The Enormous Difficulty," and a major influence on the "Outsiders" in the last chapter.

The teaching, writing, and personal witness of moral theologian Charles E. Curran at Southern Methodist University have played a major role in my life and ministry. My liberation from legalism and casuistry must be traced to professor Curran in my years of graduate work at Catholic University.

When asked the name of the five most Christlike people I have met in my life, Richard Foster is always on the list.

To John Eames and James Bryan Smith, who devoted hours to reading the manuscript and who offered valuable insights.

To the many people who have written to me, saying in effect, "Don't stop writing," I extend my heartfelt gratitude. And to Philip Yancey, whose heart is bigger and better than the best of his books.

And last, but not least, to Kathy Reigstad, whose skillful and sensitive copyediting shaped *Ruthless Trust* into a more coherent and graceful book than I had written.

1

THE WAY OF TRUST

This book started writing itself with a remark from my spiritual director. "Brennan, you don't need any more insights into the faith," he observed. "You've got enough insights to last you three hundred years. The most urgent need in your life is to trust what you have received."

That sounded simple enough. But his remark sparked a searing reexamination of my life, my ministry, and the authenticity of my relationship with God—a reexamination that spanned the next two years. The challenge to actually trust God forced me to deconstruct what I had spent my life constructing, to stop clutching what I was so afraid of losing, to question my personal investment in every word I had ever written or spoken about Jesus Christ and fearlessly to ask myself if I trusted him.

Through countless hours of silence, solitude, soul-searching, and prayer, I learned that the act of trust is an utterly ruthless act.

The film *Chariots of Fire* won the Oscar in 1981 as the best movie of the year. It dramatized the story of two British runners, Eric Liddell and Harold Abrahams, who captured gold medals in the 1924 Olympics. Heavy underdogs, the pair triumphed through a remarkable display of character, discipline, and courage. One scene in the film moved me in a profound way:

Lidell, an uncompromising Scottish Congregationalist, has been called by God to serve as a missionary in China at the conclusion of the games. However, his deeply religious sister fears that if her brother wins the gold, he will be so enamored of the fame and glory of an Olympic victory that he will opt out of his missionary vocation. On the eve of the race she pleads fervently with him not to run.

He looks at her with great affection and says, "But God made me fast, and when I run I feel his pleasure."

The underlying premise of this book: the splendor of a human heart which trusts that it is loved gives God more pleasure than Westminster Cathedral, the Sistine Chapel, Beethoven's Ninth Symphony, Van Gogh's *Sunflowers,* the sight of ten thousand butterflies in flight, or the scent of a million orchids in bloom.

Trust is our gift back to God, and he finds it so enchanting that Jesus died for love of it.

A venerable spiritual mentor, Paul de Jaegher, penned these words:

> Trust is that rare and priceless treasure that wins us the affection of our heavenly Father. For him it has both charm and fascination. Among his countless children, whom he so greatly loves and whom he heaps with tenderness and favors, there are few indeed, who truly entrusting themselves to him, live as veritable children of God. There are as few who respond to his goodness by a trust at once filial and unshaken. And so it is that he welcomes with a love of predilection those souls, all too few in number, who in adversity as in joy, in tribulation and consolation, unfalteringly trust in his paternal love. Such souls truly delight and give immense pleasure to the heart of their heavenly Father. There is nothing he is not prepared to give them. "Ask of me half of my Kingdom" he cries to the trusting soul, and "I will give it to you.[1]

Unwavering trust is a rare and precious thing because it often demands a degree of courage that borders on the heroic. When the shadow of Jesus' cross falls across our lives in the form of failure, rejection, abandonment, betrayal, unemployment, loneliness, depression, the loss of a loved one; when we are deaf to everything but the shriek of our own pain; when the world around us suddenly seems a hostile, menacing place—at those times we may cry out in anguish, "How could a loving God permit this to happen?" At such moments the seeds of distrust are sown. It requires heroic courage to trust in the love of God no matter what happens to us.

The most brilliant student I ever taught in seminary was a young man named Augustus Gordon. He now lives as a hermit six months each year in a solitary cabin deep in the Smoky Mountains above Liberty, Tennessee. The remaining half-year he travels the country preaching the gospel on behalf of Food for the Poor, a missionary outreach feeding the hungry and homeless in Haiti, Jamaica, and other Caribbean islands.

On a recent visit I asked him, "Gus, could you define the Christian life in a single sentence?" He didn't even blink before responding. "Brennan," he said, "I can define it in a single word: trust."

It has been more than four decades since I was first ambushed by Jesus in a little chapel in the Allegheny Mountains of western Pennsylvania. After thousands of hours of prayer and meditation over the intervening years, I can state unequivocally that childlike surrender in trust is the defining spirit of authentic discipleship. And I would add that the supreme need in most of our lives is often the most overlooked—namely, the need for an uncompromising trust in the love of God. Furthermore, I would say that, while there are times when it is good to go to God as might a ragged beggar to the King of kings, it is vastly superior to approach God as a little child would approach his or her papa.

In first-century Palestine the question dominating religious discussion was, How do we hasten the advent of the Kingdom of God? Jesus proposed a single way: *the way of trust.* He never *asked* his disciples to trust in God. Rather, he *demanded* of them bluntly, "Trust in God and trust in me" (John 14:1). Trust was not some feature out at the edges of Jesus' teaching; it was its heart and center. This and only this would bring on speedily the reign of God.

When the brilliant ethicist John Kavanaugh went to work for three months at "the house of the dying" in Calcutta, he was seeking a clear answer as to how best to spend the rest of his life. On the first morning there he met Mother Teresa. She asked, "And what can I do for you?" Kavanaugh asked her to pray for him.

"What do you want me to pray for?" she asked. He voiced the request that he had borne thousands of miles from the United States: "Pray that I have clarity."

She said firmly, "No, I will not do that." When he asked her why, she said, "Clarity is the last thing you are clinging to and must let go of." When Kavanaugh commented that *she* always seemed to have the clarity he longed for, she laughed and said, "I have never had clarity; what I have always had is trust. So I will pray that you trust God."[2]

"We ourselves have known and put our trust in God's love toward ourselves" (1 John 4:16). Craving clarity, we attempt to eliminate the risk of trusting God. Fear of the unknown path stretching ahead of us destroys childlike trust in the Father's active goodness and unrestricted love.

We often presume that trust will dispel the confusion, illuminate the darkness, vanquish the uncertainty, and redeem the times. But the crowd of witnesses in Hebrews 11 testifies that this is not the case. Our trust does not bring final clarity on this earth. It does not still the chaos or dull the pain or provide a crutch. When all else is unclear, the heart of trust says, as Jesus did on the cross, "Into your hands I commit my spirit" (Luke 23:46).

If we could free ourselves from the temptation to make faith a mindless assent to a dusty pawnshop of doctrinal beliefs, we would discover with alarm that the essence of biblical faith lies in trusting God. And, as Marcus Borg has noted, "The first is a matter of the head, the second a matter of the heart. The first can leave us unchanged, the second intrinsically brings change."[3]

The faith that animates the Christian community is less a matter of believing in the existence of God than a practical trust in his loving care under whatever pressure. The stakes here are enormous, for I have not said in my heart, "God exists," until I have said, "I trust you." The first assertion is rational, abstract, a matter perhaps of natural theology, the mind laboring at its logic. The second is "communion, bread on the tongue from an unseen hand."[4] Against insurmountable obstacles and without a clue as to the outcome, the trusting heart says, "Abba, I surrender my will and my life to you without any reservation and with boundless confidence, for you are my loving Father."

Though we often disregard our need for an unfaltering trust in the love of God, that need is the most urgent we have. It is the remedy for much of our sickness, melancholy, and self-hatred. The heart converted from mistrust to trust in the irreversible forgiveness of Jesus Christ is redeemed from the corrosive power of fear. The existential dread that salvation is reserved solely for the proper and pious, the nameless fear that we are predestined to backslide, the brooding pessimism that the good news of God's love is simply wishful thinking—all these combine to weave a thin membrane of distrust that keeps us in a chronic state of anxiety.

The decisive (or what I call the *second*) conversion from mistrust to trust—a conversion that must be renewed daily—is the moment of sovereign deliverance from the warehouse of worry. So life-changing is this ultimate act of confidence in the acceptance of Jesus Christ that it can properly be called the hour of salvation. So often what is notoriously missing from the external, mechanized concept of salvation is *self-acceptance*, an experience that is internally personalized and rooted in the acceptance of Jesus Christ. It bids good riddance to unhealthy guilt, shame, remorse, and self-hatred. Anything less—self-rejection in any form—is a manifest sign of a lack of trust in the total sufficiency of Jesus' saving work. Has he set me free from fear of the Father and dislike of myself, or has he not?

The grace-laden act of trust is the landmark decision of life outside of which nothing has value and inside of which every relationship and achievement, every success and failure derives its final meaning. Unbounded trust in the merciful love of the redeeming God deals a mortal blow to skepticism, cynicism, self-condemnation, and despair. It is our decisive *YES* to Christ's command, "Trust in God and trust in me."

The words of the fifteenth-century theologian Angelus Silesius, "If God stopped thinking of me, he would cease to exist," are thoroughly orthodox. Silesius merely paraphrases the message of Jesus: "Can you not buy five sparrows for two pennies? And yet not one is forgotten in God's sight. Why, every hair on your head has been counted. There is no need to be afraid; you are worth more than hundreds of sparrows" (Luke 12:6–7).

God, by definition, is thinking of me.

The merchant of mistrust dismisses these words as hyperbole and remains grim, sullen, fearful. The trusting disciple receives them and has an attack of the happies.

THE BASIC PREMISE of biblical trust is the conviction that God wants us to grow, to unfold, and to experience fullness of life. However, this kind of trust is acquired only gradually and most often through a series of crises and trials. Through the indescribable anguish on Mount Moriah with his son Isaac, Abraham learned that the God who had called him to hope against hope was eminently reliable and that the only thing expected of him was unconditional trust. The great old man models the essence of trust in the Hebrew and Christian scriptures: to be convinced of the reliability of God.

The story of salvation-history indicates that without exception trust must be purified in the crucible of trial. David, the most beloved figure of Jewish history, was no stranger to terror, loneliness, failure, and even sinister plots to destroy him; yet he ravished the heart of God with his unwavering trust.

> "When I am most afraid, I put my trust in you; in God whose word I praise, in God I put my trust, fearing nothing; what can men do to me?" (Ps. 56:3–4).
>
> "My trust in God never wavers" (Ps. 26:1).
>
> "He rescued me, since he loves me" (Ps. 18:19).
>
> "But I for my part rely on your love, O Lord" (Ps. 13:5).
>
> "Put your trust in Yahweh, be strong, let your

heart be bold, put your trust in Yahweh" (Ps. 27:14).

"Happy the man who puts his trust in Yahweh" (Ps. 40:4).

"I mean to thank you constantly for doing what you did, and put my trust in your name, that is so full of kindness, in the presence of those who love you" (Ps. 52:9).

"I, for my part, like an olive tree growing in the house of God, put my trust in God's love for ever and ever" (Ps. 52:8).

Behold the splendor of a human heart which trusts that it is loved!

Perhaps it is no coincidence that the apostle John has come to be known as the *beloved* disciple. Why? "We ourselves have known and put our trust in God's love toward ourselves" (1 John 4:16a). David and John, soul-mates, singing the same lyrical song of unfaltering trust in the love of God!

I will never forget the witness of an Episcopal priest named Tom Minifie several years ago in St. Luke's Church in Seattle, Washington. He spotted a high-profile couple sitting in the last pew with their one-year-old Down's syndrome child. It was clear from the parents' demeanor that the little one embarrassed them. They hid in the rear of the church, perhaps planning a hasty exit once the worship service had concluded.

On their way out the door, Tom intercepted them

and said, "Come into my office." Once seated, Tom took the Down's baby in his arms and rocked him gently. Looking into the baby's face, he began to sob. "Do you have any idea of the gift that God has given you in this child?" he asked.

Sensing confusion and even concern in the parents, he explained his reaction: "Two years ago my three-year-old daughter, Sylvia, died with Down's syndrome. We have four other children, so we know the blessing that kids can be. Yet the most precious gift we've ever received in our entire lives has been Sylvia. In her uninhibited expression of affection, she revealed to us the face of God as no other human being ever has. Did you know that several Native American tribes attribute divinity to Down's children because in their utter simplicity they're a transparent window into the Great Spirit? Treasure this child, for he will lead you into the heart of God."

From that day forward the parents began to brag about their little one.

Uncompromising trust in the love of God inspires us to thank God for the spiritual darkness that envelops us, for the loss of income, for the nagging arthritis that is so painful, and to pray from the heart, "Abba, into your hands I entrust my body, mind, and spirit and this entire day—morning, afternoon, evening, and night. Whatever you want of me, *I* want of me, falling into you and trusting in you in the midst of my life. Into your heart I entrust my heart, feeble, distracted, insecure, uncertain. Abba, unto you I abandon myself in Jesus our Lord. Amen."

In the arc of my unremarkable life, wherein the victories have been small and personal, the trials fairly pedestrian, and the failures large enough to deeply wound me and those I love, I have repeated endlessly the pattern of falling down and getting up, falling down and getting up. Each time I fall, I am propelled to renew my efforts by a blind trust in the forgiveness of my sins from sheer grace, in the acquittal, vindication, and justification of my ragged journey based not on any good deeds I have done (the approach taken by the Pharisee in the temple) but on an unflagging trust in the love of a gracious and merciful God.

When Roslyn and I married, we were both unemployed. My ministry had been shut down in the Catholic Church, and I was virtually unknown in other ecclesial communities. Offers to preach the gospel went a-begging, and the knock on the door never came.

Our story is perhaps a paradigm for every trusting disciple. The way of trust is a movement into obscurity, into the undefined, into ambiguity, not into some predetermined, clearly delineated plan for the future. The next step discloses itself only out of a discernment of God acting in the desert of the present moment. The reality of naked trust is the life of a pilgrim who leaves what is nailed down, obvious, and secure, and walks into the unknown without any rational explanation to justify the decision or guarantee the future. Why? Because God has signaled the movement and offered it his presence and his promise.

Of course there were days when I was afraid, when my heart sank and my body trembled, when I felt muddled and befuddled, when I felt like a bewildered child alone and lost in the dark night, hearing strange and frightening noises; put simply, there were days when anxiety and uncertainty prevailed. Then out of nowhere came a calm, reassuring voice, "Do not be afraid. I am with you."

The biggest obstacle on my journey of trust has been an oppressive sense of insecurity, inadequacy, inferiority, and low self-esteem. I have no memory of being held, hugged, or kissed by my mother as a little boy. I was called a nuisance and a pest and told to shut up and be still. My mother had been orphaned at age three—both her parents died in a flu epidemic in Montreal—and sent to an orphanage where she lived for several years, until she was eventually adopted. Then, at age eighteen, she moved to Brooklyn, New York, for training as a registered nurse. Having received little attention or affection through those early years, she was incapable of giving any.

In his later years, my father became the kindest, gentlest man I have ever known. But when I was a child, he was never there. Burdened with the limitations of an eighth-grade education, he sought work futilely and frantically during the Great Depression. I could not understand why he was never around (except to speak a word of correction or to impose physical discipline). When I saw kids my own age enjoying a great relationship with their moms and dads, I concluded that there must be something missing in me. It was *my* fault. Because I constantly blamed myself, the seed of a corrosive self-hatred took root. In the absence of any expression of attention or affection on the part of others, I found it unthinkable that God might have tender feelings for me.

One snowy night when I was six years old, my father returned home from a hard day of job-hunting and asked my mother how we boys had behaved. Pointing to my brother, Rob (fifteen months older than I), she said, "He's incorrigible. I want you to march him down to the police station right now. Tell the cops to put him in jail and leave him there."

And my father did just that. I knelt on the broad windowsill with my nose pressed against the glass, hoping against hope that my brother would return. Half an hour later, my father came walking up the street alone. The terror of rejection and abandonment gripped my heart. Tears rolled down my cheeks. Trembling, I realized that there was no one to protect me. I was utterly alone. I knew that I would be next.

Then I saw Rob about thirty yards behind my father. He was making a snowball. The inner panic subsided a bit, though I was still scared and shaken. Wiping the tears from my eyes, I climbed down from the sill, assumed the macho position of a little-boys-don't-cry six-year-old, and pretended disinterest in a traumatic event that haunted me for years.

But there is more. One morning in prayer—I was an adult by this time—I had a vivid image of my now deceased mother at age six in the orphanage, kneeling on the windowsill, her nose pressed against the glass, tears streaming down her face as she begged God to send two nice people who would adopt her. Suddenly all the anger simmering within me at my mother, all the resentment I had felt because she hadn't been there for me as a child, disappeared. Sobbing, I asked her forgiveness. With a radiant smile she said, "I may have messed up, but you turned out okay." As she hugged and kissed me, the greatest enemy of trust in my life was disarmed.

Wallowing in shame, remorse, self-hatred, and guilt over real or imagined failings in our past lives betrays a distrust in the love of God. It shows that we have not accepted the acceptance of Jesus Christ and thus have rejected the total sufficiency of his redeeming work. Preoccupation with our past sins, present weaknesses, and character defects gets our emotions churning in self-destructive ways, closes us within the mighty citadel of self, and preempts the presence of a compassionate God. From personal experience I can testify that the language of low self-esteem is harsh and demanding; it abuses, accuses, criticizes, rejects, finds fault, blames, condemns, reproaches, and scolds in a monologue of impatience and chastisement.

Rather than being surprised that we have done anything good—as certainly we have—we are shocked and horrified that we have failed. We would never judge any of God's other children with the savage condemnation with which we crush ourselves. Indeed, self-hatred becomes bigger than life itself, growing until it is seen as the beginning and the end. The image of the childhood story about Chicken Little comes to mind. In our self-hatred, we feel that the sky is falling.

Understandably, then, we hide our true selves from God in prayer. We simply do not trust that he can handle all that goes on in our minds and hearts. Can he accept our hateful thoughts, our cruel fantasies, and our bizarre dreams? we wonder. Can he cope with our primitive images, our inflated illusions, and our exotic mental castles? We conclude that he cannot and thus withhold from Jesus what is most in need of his healing touch.[5]

In order to grow in trust, we must allow God to see us and love us precisely as we are. The best way to do that is through prayer. As we pray, the unrestricted love of God gradually transforms us. We open ourselves to receive our own truth in the light of God's truth. The Spirit opens our eyes to see what really is, to pierce through illusions so that we can discover we are seen by God with a gaze of love.

In November, 1999, as I walked across the campus of Stanford University in Palo Alto, California, toward an auditorium where I was scheduled to speak, a student approached me and said, "I like your voluminous, baggy jeans. For an old goat, you're cool, man." With in-your-face mock indignation I responded, "If you ain't cool, what's the point of going on? I mean, give me one good reason you should go slogging through the molasses of this dark, dreary, dismal world if you ain't cool. Can you imagine what it's like to be uncool in a cool world?"

He said, with some alarm, "Geez, it ain't *that* bad, man. Why don't you go talk to the chaplain?"

When I revealed my identity, he laughed. I invited him to the auditorium to listen to my lecture on the love of God, and to my surprise and delight he came. Later that night, as we walked back to his dormitory, he said that he felt distant from God.

"The academic load is heavy here," he explained. "I used to have a vibrant prayer life in high school, but I've gotten so busy here with studies, fraternity life, and wanting to fit in that I've grown careless in my relationship with God. I miss him." The young man wiped away tears with a surreptitious gesture. "I want to feel his presence. Life in the fast lane keeps me so distracted that sometimes I wonder if I trust in God at all. Then I get scared. But I keep doing the same stuff out of habit because I can't imagine any other alternative. I wish I were closer to God."

The following morning a faculty member came to visit me. Her words sounded almost like a replay of the student's sharing the previous night. "At one point in my life," she said, "I had a faith so strong that it shaped the very fiber of each day. I was conscious of God's presence even in stressful situations. The fire of Christ burned inside me. Slowly, though, and almost imperceptibly, I stopped sitting at the fireplace. The academic competition is fierce here, all-consuming." With an expressive sigh she sank back in her chair.

After a moment she continued: "After you spoke on the love of God last night, I cried for an hour. My life is so empty. I see so much pain and suffering both on and off campus, and sometimes I feel a deep resistance to a loving God. I still have faith—I *know* I do—but I can't *feel* it; I've lost any sense of God's presence. I'm like Mary Magdalene in the garden, crying, 'Where has my Beloved gone?' I miss God so much that sometimes I feel frantic. I long for the relationship I used to have."

Now look at this student and this faculty member and pretend that you are the God of love bodied forth in Jesus of Nazareth. The young man is sad because he misses you, downcast that he is not closer to you, grieving because he has gotten so busy that he has neglected you, and close to panic that he does not trust in your love anymore.

The woman is in tears because she cannot feel your presence as she once did. Her heartache lies in experiencing your absence. Ambushed by academia, she fears that her faith is fading and that she has lost you forever.

Still supposing that you are God for a moment, what are your feelings toward these two? Do you see them as having a relationship with you? Do you think that they love you? Is your heart overflowing with compassion for their feelings of exile from you? Do you see their whole life as a prayer of longing? Will you sweep them up in your arms the moment they call to you?

Take your human feelings, multiply them exponentially into infinity, and you will have a hint of the love of God revealed by and in Jesus Christ. With a strong affirmation of our goodness and a gentle understanding of our weakness, God is loving us—you and me—this moment, just as we are and not as we should be. There is nothing any of us can do to increase his love for us and nothing we can do to diminish it.

When we get waylaid from our walk with God by busyness, depression, family problems, or worse, God does not abandon us. Nor, if we walk the way of trust, do we abandon God. When we wander off the path, that trust pulls us back; and we do not flinch, hesitate, or worry about being unwelcome in the Father's arms. No matter where we are on the journey, we have a quiet confidence that our trust in God's love gives God immense pleasure.

However, if we picture God as touchy, unapproachable, and easily annoyed, if we image God as haughty, indifferent, or angry, if we invest him with unlovable qualities and cringe before his glance, we will dismiss the way of trust as a chimera, a cul-de-sac, or a soft, easy path for wimps and wusses. Our skepticism, cynicism, or triumphant rationalism will banish the Beyond-in-our-midst to outer space, a Being aloof and disengaged from the joys and struggles of his children.

In the 1930s Daniel Considine wrote, "Never was a mother so blind to the faults of her child as our Lord is toward ours."[6] Therefore, we should never be discouraged by our faults. We can begin by not being astonished at them. A little child who does not know how to walk is not astonished at stumbling and falling with each step taken. While the gravity of sin is not to be minimized, wasting time deploring the past keeps God at a distance. As the second-century shepherd of Hermas said, "Stop harping on your sins and pray for righteousness."

Of what avail is our life of prayer, our study of scripture, theology, and spirituality, if we do not trust the insights that we have received? Waffling back and forth between a decisive *yes* and a discouraging *no* keeps us in a state of terminal procrastination. Likewise, an exclusive emphasis on the burning theological issues of the day (many of which are neither burning nor theological) or a one-sided emphasis on the pressing issues of social justice can temporarily or even permanently postpone a decision to trust in the love of God, thus keeping us in a state of spiritual limbo.

"To live without risk is to risk not living," my paternal grandma used to say. The way of trust is risky business, no doubt about it. To change careers suddenly because one feels unfulfilled, to assume the energy-depleting care of elderly parents, to retreat for three days of silence and solitude with Jesus without climbing the walls, to volunteer for a summer in the sub-Sahara with only meager spiritual resources, to take an unpopular position with rumblings of fear in the background, to conquer disillusionment when one finds untrustworthiness where least expected—all these challenges require a willingness to risk a journey into the unknown and a readiness to trust God even in the darkness.

A person should not act impulsively, of course. A careful discernment process involving family, friends, and a spiritual mentor should precede every major decision. But when the appropriate time comes, only the disciple with an unflinching trust in God will dare to risk. And that trust is not naïve; it knows that the possibility of making a mistake and getting hurt is very real. But without exposure to potential failure, there is no risk.

In explaining the growth of his faith, psychiatrist Gerald May writes, "I know that God is loving and that God's loving is trustworthy. I know this directly, through the experience of my life. There have been plenty of times of doubt, especially when I used to believe that trusting God's goodness meant I would not be hurt. But having been hurt quite a bit, I know God's goodness goes deeper than all pleasure and pain—it embraces them both."[7]

Naturally, the risk-takers are unnerving to the palace guards, who are threatened by anyone who trusts in God rather than the law. The latter tend to despise men and women who are not as cautious as they. They elevate themselves above the sinner and the nonconformist. Because of this reliance on self, coupled with a lack of self-knowledge, the legalists render themselves incapable of receiving grace; they do not and dare not live by trust in a loving God. They shake their heads, invoke hallowed traditions, and gratuitously employ their most potent and cruel weapon: guilt-tripping. Threatened by the freedom of anyone who trusts in God rather than the law, legalists warn of dire consequences and howl like a wolf pack in the night.

The disciple, however, no longer plagued by the desire to please others and valuing God's approval more than the disapproval of humans, moves on with eyes fixed on Jesus, "the author and pioneer of our trust" (Heb. 12:2).

I FOUND HENRI NOUWEN'S most recent book fascinating. In *The Inner Voice of Love,* a relatively brief (115-page) book published on the day of his death, Nouwen uses the word *trust* or *trusting* sixty-five times. Some examples: "At every moment you have to decide to trust the voice that says, 'I love you. I knot you together in your mother's womb' (Ps. 139:13)"; "Stop wandering around. Instead, come home and trust that God will bring you what you need"; "For as long as you can remember, you have been a pleaser, depending on others to give you an identity. But now you are being asked to let go of all these self-made props and trust that God is enough for you"; "The root choice is to trust at all times that God is with you and will give you what you most need."[8]

Nouwen's earlier books are peppered with the word *faith*. And yet in his swan song, he uses *faith* once and *trust* sixty-five times. My point? Somewhere along the way, in the life of the maturing Christian, faith combined with hope (more on this later) grows into trust. Based on the lived experience of God's relentless faithfulness, a confidence blossoms that God is with us to continue and finish what he started. So unwavering was this trust in Nouwen's life that he envisioned his own death as a happy experience. Of this I am convinced.

And I suspect that fidelity to the way of trust will lead us to the same place it took Job: "Even though he slay me, yet will I trust him" (Job 13:15, KJV).

2 

THE WAY OF GRATEFULNESS

Let's say I interviewed ten people, asking each the same question—"Do you trust God?"—and each answered, "Yes, I trust God," but nine of the ten actually did *not* trust him. How would I find out which one of the ragamuffins was telling the truth?

I would videotape each of the ten lives for a month and then, after watching the videos, pass judgment using this criterion: the person with an abiding spirit of gratitude is the one who trusts God.

The foremost quality of a trusting disciple is gratefulness. Gratitude arises from the lived perception, evaluation, and acceptance of all of life as grace—as an undeserved and unearned gift from the Father's hand. Such recognition is itself the work of grace, and acceptance of the gift is implicitly an acknowledgment of the Giver.

The grateful heart cries out in the morning, "Thank you, Lord, for the gift of a new day." And it continues to express its gratitude as the blessings unfold:

> Thank you for the gift of loving and being loved, for the beauty of the animals on the farm and in the forest, for the sound of a waterfall, for the darting beauty of the trout in the brook.
>
> Thank you for the deer leaping across the meadow, for fire and water and the magic of Monet, for the rainbow after a summer storm, for a woman with windblown hair striding down the hillside, and for a steaming cup of hot coffee.
>
> Thank you for the smile on the face of a little child licking a chocolate ice-cream cone, for the wagging tail of a dog and the touch of his cold nose against my face.
>
> Thank you that I was born in that house on East 48th Street in Brooklyn and not in the house next door, for had my birthplace been different, I might never have met Jesus and the many beautiful people I know through him.
>
> Thank you for the four seasons, for each glorious day of sunshine, and most of all for the gift of the Unsetting Sun, Jesus Christ, who by his death and resurrection has set us on the road to glory.

I shall never forget reading Jacques Maritain's *Seven Essays on Metaphysics* during my undergraduate days at St. Francis seminary in Loretto, Pennsylvania. In one of those essays, Maritain tells of one day finding himself—a world-renowned, seventy-seven-year-old philosopher—skipping across a hilltop in Toulouse, France, and shouting to the heavens, "I'm alive; I'm alive!" Having experienced sudden and utterly surprising rapture at the gift of life, the joy of being invested with existence, the privilege of *being* rather than *not being,* Maritain sank to his knees whispering words of praise and thanksgiving.

The rediscovery of the precious gift of life and existence, often taken for granted, gives birth to the spirit of gratefulness; the awareness of contingency, forcefully presented by the evening news, prods the decision to accept the invitation to celebrate the feast of life one day at a time. Coupled with an intermittent awareness of the divine Indwelling, Jesus' words "I have come so that you may have life and have it to the full" (John 10:10) sparkle with the sense that life is to be cherished infinitely.

Sitting on my desk is a picture of me, cradling in my arms one-week-old Eloise Grace Elford, the daughter of a dear friend, born in Surrey, England, at seven pounds and fourteen ounces. From the seed of her parents and the kiss of God's mouth, she rocketed into human history, lavishly enriched with the gift of life, and presented the three of us (the usual suspects—her mother and father—were also in the room) with a smile that fairly shouted, "I am! It is sooooo good to be alive."

Swiss theologian Hans Urs von Balthasar states, "We need only to know who and what we really are to break into spontaneous praise and thanksgiving." Scarred and screwed-up though we are, an appreciation of our greatness as Abba's beloved child, vibrantly alive in Christ Jesus, overcomes the sleazy sense of our seedy self and elicits the grateful exclamation, "I thank you, Lord, for the wonder of myself" (Ps. 139:14).

Here we may find the explanation for why the great saints spoke frequently about their sinfulness. Motivated not by masochism, false modesty, or low self-esteem, but by gratitude, they grew into an ever-deepening awareness that their passion for Christ, their heroic life of prayer, and their unstinting generosity in ministry were all unmerited gifts. They also grew to realize how often they forgot their giftedness. The parable of the merciless debtor clearly states that we sin against God if we fail to forgive the petty grievances of our neighbor. But the truth is that we sin every day, whenever we fail to be grateful to God for his manifold gifts.

Was the primal sin of Adam and Eve ingratitude? Is it possible that God is more interested in the gratitude of our hearts than in anything else? The parable of the ten lepers (Luke 16:11–19) lends support to this surmise.

In 1996, George Gallup Jr. wrote a book entitled, *The*

Saints Among Us. A committed Christian and devout Episcopalian, this famous poll-taker identified true holiness with seemingly ordinary people located among segments of the population that are poor, minimally educated, and non-white. Asked what this identification implies, Gallup answered:

> In many cases there are people who have known dire economic straits, yet their trust has enabled them to step outside their grim conditions and to find joy in life, so they run against the grain. The fact that they are downscale suggests that though they are burdened by economic problems, they are not overcome by them. They are more forgiving, more grateful and more likely to be unprejudiced, as well as twice as likely to be involved in outreach to neighbors, as persons at the lower end of the spiritual commitment scale. In other studies we have done, such as financial giving, we found that the poor give a larger proportion of their income to charity than the rich. Being surrounded by misery, they see opportunities to help on every side. The rich, especially now, with the widening gap between rich and poor, have a tendency to cordon themselves off and therefore don't see much of the grimness of life.[1]

Should you spend any time with older black women in the Deep South (New Orleans, for instance), you could not help but notice how often they say, "Thank you, Jesus," throughout the day.

The Pharisee of the temple (Luke 18:9–14) on the other hand, is estranged from the spirit of gratefulness. He is indignant that Jesus would care about sinners, incensed that he would befriend the rabble. The prime fault of this Pharisee, a self-righteous man who condemns sinners as unrighteous, is his belief in his faultlessness. Conscious of his religiosity, he expresses thanks only for what he has and is; he is blinded to what he has not and is not. What Jesus says, in effect, to this enemy of the gospel of grace is this: These people you despise are real sinners not because they missed their morning meditation but because their professions have debased them, lust and greed have ensnared them. However, they have sincerely repented and now have what you lack—a deep gratitude to God for his mercy and goodness.

Underlying every cry of the grateful sinner is an unshaken trust in the person and promise of Jesus. Jesus' parables of the sheer gratuity of grace rustle like refreshing rain on the parched ground of pharisaical piety, sweep like a wild storm into the glum corners of sentimental hallelujah religion, and vibrate like sharp lightning in the sulfurous atmosphere of legalists hell-bent on nonhistorical orthodoxy.

We read in the New Testament stories that illuminate the concept of grace. We hear about the eleventh-hour workers in the vineyard and the prodigious generosity of the landowner (Matt. 20:1–16), the scruffy tax-collector who goes home acquitted (Luke 18:10–14), the beggars, cripples, blind, and lame who are given reserved seats at the messianic banquet (Luke 14:16–24), the ragged, wretched prodigal son and his prodigal father, who scandalizes the trivial, calculating spirit of manhandled religion (Luke 15:11–32). Then we are introduced to the God revealed by and in Jesus Christ, who is incomparably Other. Uncontaminated trust in the revelation of Jesus allows us to breathe more freely, to dance more joyfully, and to sing more gratefully about the gift of salvation.

TO WALK IN GRATITUDE is a way of living that is inclusive, attentive, contagious, and theocentric. Let's look at each of these traits in turn.

Gratitude is inclusive. At an A.A. meeting in Kinsale, Ireland, a man named Tony said, "If I had to choose among all the diseases that afflict human beings, I would choose mine [alcoholism], because I can do something about it." At that meeting (as at each meeting) he introduced himself as "a grateful recovering alcoholic." When asked why, he said, "Because without the Twelve Steps of this program I never would have found God." Likewise, in the Book of Job, that ruined man of God said, "If we take happiness from God's hand, must we not take sorrow too?" (Job 1:10).

The sorely missed Henri Nouwen wrote of the spiritual work of gratitude:

> To be grateful for the good things that happen in our lives is easy, but to be grateful for all of our lives—the good as well as the bad, the moments of joy as well as the moments of sorrow, the successes as well as the failures, the rewards as well as the rejections—that requires hard spiritual work. Still, we are only grateful people when we can say thank you to all that has brought us to the present moment. As long as we keep dividing our lives between events and people we would like to remember and those we would rather forget, we cannot claim the fullness of our beings as a gift of God to be grateful for. Let's not be afraid to look at everything that has brought us to where we are now and *trust* that we will soon see in it the guiding hand of a loving God.[2]

Yes, gratitude is inclusive. As psychoanalyst Eric Erikson once noted, there are only two choices: integration and acceptance of our whole life-story, or despair. Thus, the apostle Paul writes, "For *all* things give thanks to God, because this is what God expects you to do in Christ Jesus" (1 Thess. 5:18).

Gratitude is attentive. When we are inwardly dissipated through busyness, obsession, addiction, mindlessness, and preoccupation with television, sports, gossip, movies, shallow reading, and so forth, we cannot be attentive to the gifts that arrive each day.

The disciple asks the guru, "What must I do to become fully enlightened?" The guru replies, "Awareness." The disciple scratches his head and asks the guru to elaborate. The guru answers, "Awareness, awareness, awareness, awareness." To be aware and alert to the presence of God manifested in a piece of music heard on the car radio, a daffodil, a kiss, an encouraging word from a friend, a thunderstorm, a newborn baby, a sunrise or sunset, a rainbow, or the magnificent lines on the face of an old lobster fisherman requires an inner freedom from self created through prayer. Gratefulness is born of a prayerfulness that helps us notice the *magnalia Dei,* the marvels of God—the crossing of the Red Sea, the pillar and fire, and so forth.

Gratitude is contagious. Grateful people are a delight to be around, and their spirit is often catching. It is simply not possible to be simultaneously grateful and resentful or full of self-pity. John Kavanaugh relates the story of a grateful old woman in an extended-care hospital:

> She had some kind of "wasting disease," her different powers fading away over the march of the month. A student of mine happened upon her on a coincidental visit. The student kept going back, drawn by the strange force of the woman's joy. Though she could no longer move her arms and legs, she would say,

"I'm just so happy I can move my neck." When she could no longer move her neck, she would say, "I'm just so glad I can hear and see."

When the young student finally asked the old woman what would happen if she lost her sound and sight, the gentle old lady said, "I'll just be so grateful that you come to visit."

There was an uncommon freedom in that student's eyes as she told me of her friend. Somehow a great enemy had been disarmed in her life.[3]

As Brother David Steindl-Rast notes, "The root of joy is gratefulness. . . . It is not joy that makes us grateful; it is gratitude that makes us joyful."[4]

Finally, gratitude is theocentric. G. K. Chesterton once remarked that the worst moment for an atheist is when he/she feels grateful and there is no one to thank. The theocentric character of gratitude is anchored in trust that there is Someone to thank. Arguably, it might be stated that the dominant theme of Jesus' inner life and prayer was gratitude. Raised in the Jewish tradition, Jesus undoubtedly thanked God before and after each meal and prayed the great thanksgiving psalms (21, 28, 30, 65, 66, 116, 136, 139) with deep gratitude for his Father's love and faithfulness. In the hymn of jubilation (Luke 10:21), he thanked his Abba "for hiding these things from the learned and the clever and revealing them to mere children. Yes, Father, that is what gave you pleasure." In the Upper Room, with the awareness of his imminent death foremost in his mind, he took some bread, and "when he had given thanks" (Luke 22:19) shared it with his disciples. Aware that his Father manifested himself in the beauty of sensible things, Jesus was grateful for the birds of the air, the lilies of the field, the sun and the moon, the hills and the valleys, the critters that roamed the countryside, and the fish that swam in the sea.

We have been given the unearned gift of salvation through no merit of ours, but by divine mercy. Our sins have been forgiven through the blood of Jesus Christ. We have received a bona fide invitation to drink new wine forever at the wedding feast in the Kingdom of God. As Jesus promised, "You will eat and drink at my table in my kingdom" (Luke 22:30).

When people realize that they have received a gift they can never repay, they notify their faces and their actions, and the tenor of their lives becomes one of humble and joyful thanksgiving. They simply rejoice in the gift. "Give thanks to the Lord, for he is good, his love is everlasting" (Ps. 107:1).

If John Henry Newman wrote a book entitled *Grammar of Assent,* it could be said that Francis of Assisi wrote a Grammar of Gratitude. His sense of thanksgiving and his utter dependence on God were not sentiment and fancy but reality and fact. In his darkest hours he still walked the way of gratefulness, devoting himself to the highest form of giving—*thanks*giving. His lyrical *Canticle of the Sun* includes even a cry of praise for "Sister Death." He knew himself to be a man possessed totally by another, belonging totally to another, and dependent totally on another.

The opposite of gratitude is, of course, ingratitude. So grievous was the matter of ingratitude in the mind of Ignatius of Loyola that he wrote a letter to Simon Rodriguez stating,

> It seems to me in the light of the Divine Goodness . . . that ingratitude is the most abominable of sins and that it should be detested in the sight of our Creator and Lord and by all of His creatures who are capable of enjoying His divine and everlasting glory. For it is a forgetting of the graces, benefits and blessings received. . . . On the contrary, the grateful acknowledgement of blessings and gifts received is loved and esteemed not only on earth but in heaven.[5]

The antithesis of giving thanks is grumbling. The grumblers live in a state of self-induced stress. Like the crew of vineyard workers who had labored from dawn to dusk and felt cheated when latecomers received the same wage (Matt. 20:1–16), they bellyache about the unfairness of life, the paucity of their gifts, the insensitivity of their spouse and employer, the liberals who are destroying the church and the conservatives who have deserted their post, the hot weather and the cold pizza, the greedy rich and the shiftless poor, and their victimization at the hands of the IRS, the Immigration and Naturalization Service, and the manufacturers of Viagra. (Small wonder that the stressed-out grumblers are two and a half times more susceptible to colds than grateful people, according to Ohio State virologist Ronald Glaser.)

In his *Rule* for monasteries, St. Benedict considered grumbling a serious offense against community life. He wrote, "If a disciple grumbles, not only aloud but in his heart . . . his action will not be accepted with favor by God, who sees that he is grumbling in his heart." Indicating his fierce opposition to this behavior, he added, "First and foremost, there must be no word or sign of grumbling, no manifestation of it for any reason at all. If, however, anyone is caught grumbling, let him undergo more severe discipline" (chapter 34).

In my mind, the most wonderful line in Benedict's *Rule* describes the appropriate response to a "contumacious monk" who is creating discord in the monastic community. "Let Father Abbot send two *stout* monks to explain the matter to him" (chapter 20, italics mine). The saintly founder of Western monasticism implies that a left jab to the solar plexus and a right hook to the jaw would swiftly clear the grousing brother's mind.

TO BE GRATEFUL for an unanswered prayer, to give thanks in a state of interior desolation, to trust in the love of God in the face of the marvels, cruel circumstances, obscenities, and commonplaces of life is to whisper a doxology in darkness.

3

THE ENORMOUS DIFFICULTY

"*Forever I will sing the goodness of the Lord*" (Ps. 89:1).

How difficult for me to sing that song when a morning phone call delivered the news that my forty-one-year-old friend Rich Mullins had been killed in a gruesome auto accident just a few hours earlier in Illinois. Without explanation I turned down several requests to speak at memorial services in his honor in Nashville, Wichita, and Chicago. I was lost in the tangled, dark, and frightening inner world of my grief, doubt, fear, and anger over Rich's death.

"*Taste and see the goodness of the Lord*" (Ps. 34:1).

How hard for Anne Donovan when she delivered a stillborn baby. She said, "Those things I had relied on—modern science, women's intuition, God's mercy—had failed, and I had nothing to hold on to." When friends offered well-meaning words of condolence such as "It was God's will. We cannot understand God's will," and told her "how privileged she should feel that now she has her very own baby angel," the only taste in her mouth was ashes.[1]

"Praise the Lord for he is good" (Ps. 135:3).

Scant praise sounded from the people of the Dominican Republic, ravaged by Hurricane Georges. Thousands dead, families shattered, tens of thousands homeless, and the economy in ruins.

No singing, tasting, and praising God's goodness for the families devastated by earthquakes in Turkey and Taiwan, victims whose grieving we heard around the world.

The ubiquitous presence of pain and suffering—unwanted, apparently undeserved, and not amenable to explanation or remedy—poses an enormous obstacle to unfailing trust in the infinite goodness of God. How does one dare to propose the way of trust in the face of raw, undifferentiated heartache, cosmic disorder, and the terror of history?

Any Christian writer who ignores these grim realities or dismisses them as inconsequential is either naïve, dishonest, or disconnected from the trust-busting anguish of many struggling seekers and believers.

When pain and suffering are conjoined with the monstrous mystery of evil, we come to a crossroads from which there is no turning back. The tsunami of high school killings in Kentucky, Oregon, and Colorado, the rampage of serial killer Rafael Resendez-Ramirez, the sexual torture spree of thirty-eight-year-old Charles Ng, which led to the murder of six men, three women, and two baby boys, the horror of the seventy-year-old mother who belatedly confessed to suffocating all of her eight children before they had reached the age of two, the mass graves of slaughtered ethnic Albanians in Kosovo—the list of evil incidents goes and on and on, impressing believers and unbelievers alike more powerfully than the presence of God.

Along with Jean-Paul Sartre, Albert Camus, Samuel Beckett, and Eugène Ionesco, many Christians have been unable to cope with what they fear the most—the loneliness and absurdity of life. They have dismissed a loving God as pure fantasy, only to be touched by the icy fingers of agnosticism and atheism. As Louis Dupré writes, "The sheer magnitude of evil that our age has witnessed in death camps, nuclear warfare and internecine tribal or racial conflicts has not raised the question how can God tolerate so much evil, but rather how the more tangible reality of evil still allows the possibility of God's existence."[2]

Pain, suffering, and evil constitute a watershed for the community of faith. Many evade the question entirely, while others attempt to substitute art, rational reflection, or philosophical speculation for guttering religious trust. Indeed, as Dupré notes, "Evil invites philosophical speculation, yet it is the cliff on which philosophy suffers shipwreck."[3] Even theology cannot provide a fix for the mother whose tiny child has just died of cancer.

The Book of Job and the psalms of lament show no interest in exculpating God from responsibility for the tragedy and misery of human existence. The psalms are raw, disturbing, and brutally honest. It is to an angry and bewildered Job that God appears and speaks, and yet God later tells the theological sophisticate Eliphaz to ask for Job's prayers, adding, "for you have not spoken truthfully about me, as has my servant Job" (Job 42:7).

In chapter 53 of his prophetic book, Isaiah speaks of the mysterious figure of the Suffering Servant, who "though despised and rejected of men" and brutally savaged has nonetheless "borne our griefs and carried our sorrows" and thereby triumphed. The Christian scriptures speak of the cross and testify that God can draw good out of the most heinous evil.

In writing of the indescribable barbarity of the Holocaust, in which six million men, women, and children were annihilated, Frederick Buechner states, "But all such explanations sound pale and inadequate before the gas chambers of Buchenwald and Ravensbruck, the ovens of Treblinka."[4]

Throughout the excruciating suffering of the human experience Jesus remains, in Raymond Nogar's striking phrase, "the Lord of the Absurd,"[5] and hope in the resurrection promise stands firm and unassailable. However, to the grief-stricken wife whose husband and three small children have just been killed by a drunken driver, reassurances of eternal life offer little solace. Likewise, Anne Donovan, after the delivery of her stillborn child, heard only mocking laughter from the heavens when a well-intentioned friend recited a saccharine poem with this gruesome message: God had looked around heaven and decided that it needed some brightening up, so he plucked a vivid flower—her stillborn baby—to cheer the place up. She said, "I just clenched my teeth to keep from saying something I'd regret."[6]

Harriet Beecher Stowe understood the depths of the human struggle when she wrote these words to a heartbroken friend: "When the heart-strings are suddenly cut, it is, I believe, a physical impossibility to feel faith or resignation; there is a revolt of the instinctive and animal system, and though we may submit to God, it is rather by constant painful effort than sweet attraction."

IN ADDITION TO the trinity of pain, suffering, and evil, add another major obstacle to unhesitating trust in the merciful love of God: the wretched witness of hard-hat

Christians with their execrable images of a malevolent God. They speak in giddy or sepulchral tones of a deity who, with malicious glee, dispatches to a fiery lake ninety percent of the people he created in his image and likeness. Equally repugnant is the deity described by the peerless Philip Yancey in his masterful book *What's So Amazing About Grace?* "I grew up with the image of a mathematical God," he recalled, "who weighed my good and bad deeds on a set of scales and always found me wanting. . . . I imagined God as a distant thundering figure who prefers fear and respect to love."[7]

Writer Paul Messbarger recalls the time he and his wife visited New Orleans for a spring vacation. Like most tourists, they roamed the French Quarter the first day. As they turned the corner onto Royal Street, a woman darted in their direction. She was dressed professionally, except for a pair of tennis shoes. With a gaudy smile she said, "I knew immediately you were saved." Flummoxed by the intrusion and unfamiliar with evangelical jargon, Paul mumbled, "I hope so."

The woman blocked their attempt to pass. "Isn't it wonderful?" she cried. "Don't you just feel the Rapture is coming?" Puzzled, the couple made no reply. The woman then referred to the rising tensions in a number of Eastern European countries that seemed to be stumbling toward chaos. She interpreted the escalation of international conflict as a sure sign of impending nuclear war—a war that would hasten the end of the world, at which point the Elect would be summoned to heaven by direct bodily transport.

Messbarger had this to say about her:

> Wrapped in the folds of an invincible complacency, this child-woman sweetly voiced a message of unspeakable filth: celebrating mass destruction because certain of us by divine decree would be carved out and lifted up to enjoy eternal happiness. And then the kicker. As I was searching for some suitably hurtful riposte, she thrust a paper into my hand and said that if we would only attend a one-hour presentation at the office of a condominium developer, we could have a free breakfast at the Court of the Two Sisters on Bourbon Street![8]

From the gross impiety of the Salem witch trials down to the blasphemous, implacable images of a vindictive deity today, terror of a merciless God has haunted many a Christian conscience, making believers distrust even motherhood, the flag, and apple pie. The bromides, platitudes, and exhortations to trust God from nominal believers who have never visited the valley of desolation are not only useless; they are textbook illustrations of unmitigated gall. Only someone who has been there, who has drunk the dregs of our cup of pain, who has experienced the existential loneliness and alienation of the human condition, dares whisper the name of the Holy to our unspeakable distress. Only that witness is credible; only that love is believable.

The enormous challenge of trust is exacerbated for those in a state of depression; those trapped in a loveless marriage, hanging together for the sake of the children but seeing no way out; those who long for a friend but seem condemned to loneliness; those who cannot make a success of anything to which they turn their hands; those who long to live a good life but feel hopelessly defeated by some vice that they lack the ability to conquer; those whose faith, prayer, and service toward God, having begun with high ideals and generous self-giving, have since become meaningless—faith no longer offering assurance and comfort, prayer enveloped in darkness, ministry reduced to perfunctory routine.

And the suffering—always we come back to the suffering. How is trust to be conjured by the three million refugees who water the roads and rice paddies with their tears; those who live in countries where to be black is not to be beautiful but to be bastard; the twenty thousand homeless living in the streets of Calcutta, who build little fires to cook scraps of scavenged goods, defecate against curbstones, and curl up against a wall to sleep; those who are destroying their bodies and souls with alcohol, crack cocaine, and heroin; those whose blood reddens the earth from Kosovo to Northern Ireland to the streets of your hometown; those children with swollen bellies in the Sudan; the twelve-year-old (and younger) prostitutes, male and female, in New York City and elsewhere; those studying in the decaying schoolhouses in Appalachia?

Perhaps the reader will suspect that I am overstating the problem, exaggerating the enormous difficulty for the sake of dramatic effect. Not for those who have walked the long and lonely road to Calvary. Not for those who have endured unbearable anguish and refused to give way to despair.

The skeptic might speak to Laura, a woman whose letter arrived in my mailbox this morning: "The one thing I long to hear from God is, 'Well done.' But I know he'll never say it to me because I'm so lazy and stupid and selfish. I'm such an ungrateful brat. I'm a total failure. Do yourself a favor, Brennan. Crumple up this letter and forget about me." The skeptic might also talk to those women who were sexually abused by their father, their uncle, or their brother as children and who are now consumed by rage, shame, impotence, and self-hatred. Or to Anne Donovan, as she held her dead baby in her arms.

For that matter, speak to me sitting on a curbstone along General Meyer Avenue here in New Orleans. I am intoxicated after a relapse with alcohol. My clothes are in tatters; I reek with rancid body odor; I am unshaven. My face and belly are bloated, my eyes bloodshot. I am clutching a fifth of Smirnoff vodka—only a few ounces left. My marriage is collapsing, my friends are near despair, and my honor is broken. My brain is scrambled, my mind a junkyard of broken promises, failed dreams, unkept resolutions.

Fifty yards behind me is the detox center of F. Edward Hebert hospital. As I take the last swig, I shudder at the pain and heartache I have caused. Going to A.A. meetings, working the Twelve Steps, talking to my sponsor, reading the Big Book, praying—these have all worked for others. Why have they not worked for me? I know I will never hear the words, "Well done, good and faithful servant."

Minor panic: no more booze. Reaching in my pocket, I find a five-dollar bill. Staggering down four blocks, I find a convenience store, still open at midnight. I buy a pint of Taaka vodka. Cheaper. I retrace my steps, weaving across the avenue to reclaim my seat on the curb. I do not want the lifesaving treatment of detox. I continue drinking. My eyes fill with tears. Now I am crying, Abba's drunken child. "Jesus, where are you?" Soon I pass out with the half-full pint resting on my chest. When I wake up the next morning, I learn that two staff members had come out on the avenue and carried me into detox.

HOW DO MEN and women "clap their hands and shout with a voice of joy to God?" (Ps. 47:2) in the midst of pain, suffering, heartache, and throbbing despair? Is it possible to endure and eventually move beyond the bleak and melancholy landscape of evil and destruction?

After Saul/Paul's conversion on the road to Damascus, Jesus said to Ananias, "I myself will show him how much he himself has to suffer for my name" (Acts 9:16). Anyone God uses significantly is always deeply wounded. It is no coincidence that the title of the latest book by Michael Ford on the life and ministry of Henri Nouwen is *Wounded Prophet.* We are, each and every one of us, insignificant people whom God has called and graced to use in a significant way. In his eyes, the high-profile ministries are no more significant than those that draw little or no attention and publicity. On the last day, Jesus will look us over not for medals, diplomas, or honors, but for scars.

Where do we take the miasma of pain, suffering, and evil? Philosophical speculation and rational reflection suffer shipwreck on the shoals of the enormous difficulty. The only territory left to explore rivets our gaze on the vast, unbounded ocean of the glory of God. Irenaeus, a disciple of the apostle John, becomes our guide in his five-volume work *Against the Heresy of Gnosticism.* The oft-quoted first clause of one compound sentence reads, "The glory of God is the human being fully alive." But the less-quoted second clause reads, "and the life of the human consists in beholding God."[9]

4

THINKING BIG

In the movie *Waking Ned Devine,* a ten-year-old boy asks the interim pastor of his church, "Do you ever see God?"

"Not directly," says the young curate, "though I get revelations."

"Does your job pay well?" inquires the boy.

"No. The rewards of my work are mostly spiritual."

Then the pastor asks the boy, "Have you ever thought about a life of service to the church?"

"Not really," he says. "I don't want to work for Someone I never see and who doesn't even pay minimum wage."

I suspect that Irenaeus had something more in mind when he spoke of beholding God in the passage quoted at the end of the previous chapter. The crux of the beholding experience lies in the contemplation of the *kabōd* (the Hebrew word for *glory*) of the Lord.

In the Bible, *kabōd* is a rich and complex theological concept with multiple shades of meaning. Starting with the Old Testament, the first and most primitive meaning is the weight of an object, its heaviness as determined on a scale. A second meaning, also found in the Old Testament, refers to material wealth. Solomon's dream at Gibeon holds this promise: "What you have not asked I shall give you too," said Yahweh, "such riches and glory *[kabōd]* as no other king ever had" (1 Kings 3:13). As part of that second meaning, the word is also used in a figurative sense, to describe someone who has achieved rank, status, prominence, power (Gen. 31:1). Even today, in American argot, we might say, of one who has attained success in career and business, "He's heavy, man."

In a later period, the Jewish community identified *kabōd* with "the 'weight,' greatness, eminence, power and authority of God."[1] The awesome majesty of God is manifested in the *magnalia Dei*.

Leaping into the present for a moment, astronomers recently announced the discovery of the first multi-planet system ever found around a star other than our own. The signals from three orbiting worlds emerged after eleven years of a two-telescope survey of the star Upsilon Andromedae, which is bright enough to see with the naked eye and is located roughly 264 trillion miles from earth. The distance boggles the mind, bends the imagination, and beggars speech.

Astrophysicists today reckon that somewhere

between twelve and fifteen billion years ago, the universe began in a stellar nursery 79.8 quintillion miles away, with an explosion of immeasurable force. What happened? Some scientists think that a neutron star, composed of iron so dense that it weighed a million tons per teaspoon, was cannibalized by a black hole, itself so dense that not even light could escape. Others think that the energy may have come from the cataclysmic collapse of a supersize star perhaps one hundred times the size of our sun.

However it occurred, the explosion was so great that many suspect it must have recreated the condition of the universe in the first millisecond after the Big Bang, when all matter existed in a weird gruel percolating at forty billion degrees. Indeed, the moment was so immense that it has shocked our notions of physics. Either the observations are wrong, or there is something out there that we have not begun to comprehend. "I'm a very troubled theorist," said one researcher.[2]

We applaud him. Astrophysicists ought to be humble; they work in a divine milieu. The manifestations of *kabōd*—the *magnalia Dei*—continue in an ever-expanding cosmos. Small wonder that ninety-four years ago the eminent biographer Canon Sheehan envisioned heaven as "the never-ending unlocking of the inner chambers of God."

The mind-boggling figure of twelve to fifteen billion years—the estimated life of our universe—reminds me of a wonderful story in the Yiddish tradition. One day Israel Schwartz asked God, "Yahweh, is it true that for you a thousand years is just a minute?"

Yahweh answered, "Yes, Izzy, that is true."

Izzy had a second question: "And Yahweh, is it true that for you a million dollars is just a penny?"

Yahweh replied, "Yes, Izzy, that also is true."

Extending his right hand with palm upturned, Izzy Schwartz said, "Yahweh, give me a penny."

And Yahweh said, "Certainly. It'll take only a minute."

Returning to the biblical understanding of *kabōd* in the Hebrew scriptures, the third and most important meaning is the glory of God appearing as a light so brilliant that Yahweh himself is rendered invisible by the brilliance (Ezek. 1:28, 3:12, 3:23, 8:4, 10:18f).[3]

When Victor Hugo described God as "a divine and terrible radiance," he used the word *terrible* not to indicate something frightening or dreadful but to imply an experience that attached a degree of unbearable intensity. In that phrase, Hugo caught not only the core meaning of *kabōd*, but the truth contained in an old Jewish epigram that says, "God is not a kindly old uncle, he is an earthquake."[4]

No human being can withstand the effulgence of *kabōd*. Thus, the glory of God conveys the sense of a deep and dazzling darkness. Moses' request to see the *kabōd Yahweh* is denied. He is told to cover his face while the glory passes, watching only as God departs: "I will make all my splendor *[kabōd]* pass before you," says Yahweh, "and in your presence I will pronounce my name. . . . You cannot see my face, for no one sees me and still lives." Yahweh also says, "Here is a place beside me. You must stand on the rock, and when my glory passes by, I will put you in a cleft of the rock and shield you with my hand as I pass by. Then I will take my hand away and you shall see the back of me; but my face is not to be seen" (Exod. 33:18–23).

Peter van Breeman quotes from the journal of Old Testament scholar Fridolin Stier: "That is the apex, the ultimate, the extreme allowed to any theology, any philosophy and any scholarship: the back of God—provided they really desire to see his face."[5]

It is beyond our ken to withstand the unbearable intensity of God's holiness, power, and grandeur. God dwells in inaccessible light (1 Tim. 6:16). It is not surprising, then, that of the many near-death experiences reported, the person almost invariably walks toward a blinding light.

"No one sees me and still lives." The suffering of St. John of the Cross lay in the sadness of the human condition, which prevented him from seeing the Beatific Vision. "Reveal Thy presence," he cried, "and may the vision of Thy beauty be my death." The Spanish mystic, intoxicated by beauty, longed to see the Source of all beauty, even knowing that it would kill him. But so what if it did? His death would be his passage into eternal life, "where I shall see you in your beauty, and You shall see me in your beauty, and my beauty will be your beauty and your beauty my beauty."[6]

In the later Old Testament writings, the *kabōd Yahweh* is revealed as God's manifest holiness, and the Israelites give glory to God by recognizing and acknowledging God's divinity.

The magnificent theme of *kabōd* reaches its culmination in the Christian scriptures, as the *kabōd* rests on the person of Jesus and he shares in the luminous brilliance of his Father. He is the Light who has come into the world. To glorify Jesus is to confess his divinity as well as his humanity. In short, Jesus is God.

The carpenter who walked the dusty roads of Galilee is "one who has been tempted in every way that we are, though he's without sin" (Heb 4:15); he is also, as the Nicene Creed stipulates, God from God, Light from Light, *Kabōd* from *Kabōd,* true God from true God, eternally begotten not made, one in being with the Father. He is more than a superior human being with an intellect keener than ours and a capacity for loving greater than ours. In his divinity Jesus is inexpressibly Other, absolutely incomparable.

Jesus is the power and wisdom and holiness of God Almighty. "In him all things were created in heaven and earth" (Col. 1:6). He is creatively present 264 trillion miles from earth on the star Upsilon Andromedae. No thought can contain him; no word can express him. He transcends all human concepts, considerations, and expectations. He is the Beyond-in-our-midst, and though in our midst, still beyond anything we can intellectualize or imagine. Jesus Christ will always be a *scandal* to the murky, immodest theory-making of the intelligentsia, because he cannot be comprehended by the rational, scientific, and finite mind.

"Anyone who has been brushed by the divine *kabōd*, cannot but adore God."[7] The only appropriate response is that of the apostle John, who laid his head on the breast of Jesus in the Upper Room. In the Book of Revelation, when John saw dimly the glory of the risen Christ, he fell on his face, prostrate in adoration.

It is of immense importance to understand that every word spoken and written about God is delivered in the language of analogy. In any divine analogy, there is a similarity between the human words used about God and the reality of God himself; there is also, however, a radical *dis*similarity. What is affirmed in one breath must be denied in the next. For example, we liken divine love to human love. The similarity induces us to think that we are getting a grip on God's love. And yet, though human love is the best image we have, it is utterly inadequate to express the love of the Infinite. Not because human love is too sugary and sentimental or because it is too passionate and emotional, but because it can never fully compare with that source whence it came—the passion-emotion love of the Totally Other.

The more we let go of our concepts and images, which always limit God, the bigger God grows and the more we approach the mystery of his indefinability. When we overlook the dissimilarity, we begin to speak with obnoxious familiarity about the Holy, make ludicrous comments such as "I could never imagine God doing such a thing," calmly predict Armageddon, glibly proclaim infallible discernment of the will of God, and trivialize God, trimming the claws of the Lion of Judah.

The most moving Christian hymn I have ever heard is a humble, self-effacing, and lyrical tribute to the ineffable mystery of *kabōd*, the glory of God:

You are beautiful beyond description
Too marvelous for words,
Too wonderful for comprehension
Like nothing ever seen or heard.
Who can grasp your infinite wisdom,
Who can fathom the depth of your love?
You are beautiful beyond description
Majesty enthroned above.
And I stand, I stand in awe of you.
I stand, I stand in awe of you.
Holy God to whom all praise is due,
I stand in awe of you.[8]

When this hymn was sung in a Pioneer church at Chichester-by-the Sea, England, last June, the body language of the worshiping community moved effortlessly and naturally into profoundly reverent postures—prostration, eyes-closed adoration, silent paraliturgical dance, and profound bowing. A tangible spirit of silent wonder, radical amazement, and affectionate awe filled the warehouse that served as a holy place.

Yet I have never in my entire life heard a homily or sermon on the glory of God shining on the face of Jesus (2 Cor. 3:18). Perhaps the reticence that contemporary preachers feel about preaching on this topic is due to the fact that we have never been brushed by the divine *kabōd*. Or perhaps we simply feel incapable of articulating the concept; we sense that to address it would plunge us and our congregations into absolute mystery. And mystery is an embarrassment to the modern mind. All that is elusive, enigmatic, hard to grasp will eventually yield to our intellectual investigation, then to our conclusive categorization—or so we would like to think. But to avoid mystery is to avoid the only God worthy of worship, honor, and praise. And it is a failure to slake the thirst of seekers and believers alike—those who reject the dignified, businesslike Rotary Club deity we chatter about on Sunday morning and search for a God worthy of awe, silent reverence, total commitment, and wholehearted trust.

Thomas Aquinas, considered the greatest theologian of the Roman Catholic tradition, never completed his master work, the *Summa Theologica.* After being brushed by the *kabōd,* he humbly confessed, "I can write no more for everything I have written is straw."[9]

In his splendid book, *The Trivialization of God,* Donald McCullough writes a bold chapter entitled "In Praise of Agnosticism." And there is wisdom in McCullough's outlook. The agnostic, neither denying nor affirming the existence of God, allows for a remote, impersonal cosmic force that is utterly unknowable. Given that stance, the agnostic is spared having to repudiate the puny, pathetic images of God that scar many a Christian heart and conscience.

How do we deal with a glimpse of God's back? What happens in the wordless, empty, but shattering collision with the glory of God that such a glimpse entails? Can we gaze even momentarily into the precipitous depths of the crushing majesty and unapproachable holiness of the living God? Do we have any inner resources at the moment when we are accosted by the Holy One, when we are brought not only in thought but in the totality of our being before the great Mystery which touches the taproot of our existence and encircles our spirit even before it is brought home to us with overwhelming force?

Immediately our credentials of independence vanish, and we cease to carry ourselves with the swagger of the executive who know what's up and has all under control; we become aware of innate poverty, our next-breath dependence, and a *numbness* that invades the roots of our littleness and realness. The awareness of what Rudolph Otto called the fundamental element in all authentic spiritual experience—*mysterium tremendum*—may lead us into total self-forgetfulness and gaping wonder that is the adoration of God, or it may induce *terror,* a deep, chilling stillness that penetrates the inner sanctum of our soul as the abyss between divine holiness and human sinfulness widens. The inspired intuition that the glory of God is absolute love—even when rejected—permits only the whispered prayer of the tax-collector: "God, be merciful to me, a sinner" (Luke 18:13).

As a precocious fourteen-year-old, the distinguished Jewish philosopher Martin Buber was tormented by the question of time. His terror before the infinity and eternity of God robbed him of any sense of being at home in the world. He wrote:

> A necessity I could not understand swept over me; I had to try again to imagine the edge of space, or its edgelessness, time with a beginning and an end or a time without beginning or end, and both were equally impossible, equally hopeless—yet there seemed to be only the choice between the one or the other absurdity. Under an irresistible compulsion I reeled from one to the other, at times so closely

> threatened with the danger of madness that I seriously thought of avoiding it by suicide.[10]

This confrontation with infinity, one dimension of the *kabōd Yahweh,* filled Buber with such terrifying dread that he wrote, "I had to let myself be thrown into that bottomless abyss, into infinity and now everything whirled. It happened thus time after time. Mathematical and physical formulae could not help me; what was at stake was the world in which one had to live and which had taken on the face of the absurd and the uncanny."[11]

Needless to say, all questions, pertinent and impertinent, find no responding voice. The scandal of God's silence in the most heartbreaking hours of our journey is perceived in retrospect as veiled, tender Presence and a passage into pure trust that is not at the mercy of the response it receives.

As the *kabōd* passes by, one is gripped, in a way previously uncomprehended, by the untouchable Otherness of God: "For my thoughts are not your thoughts, my ways not your ways—it is Yahweh who speaks. Yes, the heavens are as high above earth as my ways above your ways, my thoughts above your thoughts" (Isa. 55:8–9).

When the shivering, shuddering, and shaking subside, we realize that phrases such as "the tenderness of the Father," "the compassion of the Son," and "the consolation of the Spirit" are only hints of the ineffable *kabōd,* that the substance of biblical trust lies in the conviction that beyond these hints is love beyond measure. We are drawn into the ever-deepening and more direct awareness of the divine incomprehensibility.[12]

Pundits have long maintained that the only person more arrogant than a newly certified physician is a newly ordained priest. At the age of twenty-nine, with the holy oils of ordination still wet on my hands, I sallied forth to teach theology at the university level. Exuding a brisk air of professional enthusiasm and a suffocating spirit of hubris, I expostulated so brilliantly on the mystery of God that after one semester, there was no mystery left. When I heard an elderly and saintly friar in the monastery comment, "The older I get, the less I understand about God," I assumed that it was his sincere attempt at modesty. Secretly, however, I pitied his shallowness. Looking back now, I shudder at my "profundity."

Without a hallowed and hallowing brush with the glory of God, I was like the Trappist monk from Holland who testified, "Twenty-one years I have prayed and meditated with the monks of the abbey, hours and hours of the day and night. And yet; was God alive for me? Was he real and living for me? I hope that I do not shock or scandalize anybody: he was really unknown to me."[13]

The novels of Chaim Potok, the Jewish author of *The Chosen, My Name Is Asher Lev, The Gift of Asher Lev, Davida's Harp,* and the *Book of Lights* (among others), have led me to a profound appreciation of the mystical tradition of the Hasidim. In terms of literary style, Jews are more creative, poetic, and imaginative than we comparatively staid and literalistic Westerners.

In the *Book of Lights,* Potok offers his lyrical description of *kabōd:*

A quality of holiness, a quality of power,
A quality of fearfulness, a quality of sublimity,
A quality of trembling, a quality of shaking,
A quality of terror, a quality of consternation,
Is the quality of the Garment of Zoharariel, YHWH,
God of Israel,
Who comes crowned to the Throne of His Glory. . .
And of no creature are the eyes able to behold it,
Not the eyes of flesh and blood, and not the eyes of
His servants.
And as for him who does behold it, or sees or glimpses it,
Whirling gyrations grip the balls of his eyes,
And the balls of his eyes . . . send forth torches of fire,
And these enkindle him and these burn him.[14]

The effects of "beholding God"—that is, contemplating the glory of the Lord—are profound and far-reaching. In the life of prayer, for example, adoration assumes a preeminent position. The aptitude to appreciate the grandeur of divine Reality, born of the brush with *kabōd,* takes pride of place and begets an Isaiah-like spirit of speechless humility and breathless amazement at the overpowering splendor of God. After the encounter, a Christian will resonate to the words of Abraham Heschel on his deathbed when he said to his friend, "Sam, never once in my life did I ask God for success or wisdom or power or fame. I asked for wonder, and he gave it to me." Confronted with the vision, however fleeting and obscure, of divine majesty, one becomes reluctant to speak and disinclined to share, because human language breaks down in the attempt to convey what can be grasped only in a nonrational, intuitive way. Intellect capitulates to mystery. Spiritual reading, meditation, and reflection on scripture inevitably yield to silent reverence. To adore is to recognize the unfathomable greatness of God and the nothingness of the adorer. In somewhat baroque language, Pere Sertillanges says, "Adoration is nonentity swooning and gladly expiring in the presence of Infinity." Baroque, yes. Diluted, no.

The human tendency toward projection—ascribing to God our thoughts, feelings, and attitudes about ourselves and others—is unmasked in all its absurdity. Distorted images and caricatures of God as vengeful, whimsical, fickle, and punitive (images that cannot fail to engender anxiety, fear, scrupulosity, and unhealthy guilt) are exposed for what they are—puny and pathetic human constructs.

The same judgment is passed on the illusion of control. When life is tranquil, relationships intact, finances secure, and physical health flourishing; when the enemy is not at the gate; when the war drums are not rattling;

when the Calvin Klein perfume advertisement for Eternity for Men seems plausible—then a sense of complacency, self-sufficiency, and personal command of one's destiny deludes and lulls us.

But the reality of *kabōd* shatters every delusion. As previous certainties desert us, we become vulnerable and open. The glory of God makes possible the primordial act of religion: the realization that we are not sufficient unto ourselves, that we have received our life and being from another. In a decision that reaches the roots of our most intimate self and demands the renunciation of belonging to that self, we freely ratify our condition as creatures. Through this fundamental act of dispossession we acknowledge the illusion of control and open ourselves to the reality of God.

The enormous difficulty of pain, suffering, and evil remains, heartache lingers, and there are certain wounds of the spirit that will never close. Unfortunately, organized religion is often of little help in times of spiritual crisis. In fact, it often makes matters worse. Any brand of religion that focuses exclusively on the supernatural and makes breezy pronouncements about the afterlife offers no comfort, consolation, or solidarity in our present suffering. The arrogance, rigidity, and blazing enthusiasm of religious fanatics who see in every hurricane and cosmic upheaval a sign that we are at the brink of apocalyptic catastrophe only alienate the shipwrecked and heartbroken.

However, a fleeting, incomplete glimpse of God's back—the obscure yet real, penetrating, and transforming experience of his incomparable glory—awakens a dormant *trust.* Something is afoot in the universe; Someone filled with transcendent brightness, wisdom, ingenuity, and power and goodness is about. In the face of overwhelming evidence to the contrary, somewhere deep down a Voice whispers, "All is well, and all will be well."

The late Karl Rahner insisted, "In the days ahead, you will be a mystic, i.e., one who has experienced God, or nothing at all." If Christianity is merely an ethic, a moral code, or a philosophy of life, it will not withstand the incursion of suffering. The graced experience of the divine *kabōd* is not something esoteric reserved for an elite few. When Thomas Merton was asked who might receive this gift, he replied, "The answer is obvious: everybody."

5

ARTISTS, MYSTICS, AND CLOWNS

Fyodor Dostoevsky passionately believed that he had embodied the soul of the Russian peasant in Marmeladov, the discharged town clerk and disgraced town drunk of *Crime and Punishment*—a clown, a buffoon, and the father of Sonia, a prostitute.

In a tavern in St. Petersburg, besotted with booze, Marmeladov engages the young rationalist Raskolnikov in conversation. Though the object of derision and mockery by the locals, Marmeladov insists that he is not to be pitied:

> But He will have pity on me Who has pity on all men, Who has understood all men and all things. He is the One. He too is the judge. He will come on that day and He will ask, "Where is the

> daughter [Sonia] who had pity upon the filthy drunkard, her earthly father, undismayed by his beastliness?" . . . He will forgive my Sonia, He will forgive, I know it.
>
> Then He will summon us. "You too come forth," He will say. He will say, "Come forth, ye drunkards, come forth, ye weak ones, come forth, ye children of shame!" And the wise and those of understanding will say: "Oh Lord, why dost Thou receive these men?" And He will say: "This is why I receive them, oh ye wise, this is why I receive them, oh ye of understanding, that not one of them believed himself to be worthy of this." And He will hold out his hands to us and we shall fall down before Him . . . and we shall weep . . . and we shall understand all things! Then we shall understand all . . . and all will understand. . . . Lord, Thy kingdom come!"[1]

Dostoevsky maintained that at the heart of Russian peasant life existed an *unshaken trust* in the unrestricted mercy of God and the all-forgiving love of Jesus Christ. The author's contemporary, Leo Tolstoy, published his classic novel *War and Peace* three years after *Crime and Punishment*. In a dialogue between the saintly Princess Mary and her brother Prince Andrew, she echoes Dostoevsky's ethos. Quoting a haunting French proverb, she says, "We should enter everyone's situation. *Tout comprendre, c'est tout pardonner*"—to understand all is to forgive all.[2] In his sovereign wisdom, God alone understands the human heart.

And what of the human heart's capacity to understand God? Here we need the help of passionate visionaries such as Dostoevsky. Sacred scripture is too important to be left exclusively to biblical scholars. Theology is too vital to be consigned solely to the province of theologians. To explore the depths of the God who invites our trust, we need the artists and mystics.

The Christian artists who composed such hymns as "How Great Thou Art," "There's a Wideness in God's Mercy," "I Stand in Awe of You," and "Taste and See the Goodness of the Lord" invite us to stretch our limited understanding of God. Through daring images and bold metaphors rooted in the Word, they guide us to a profound self-esteem within an enlarged vision of the magnitude of the Divine. In Karl Rahner's words, they help us in "coming to see ourselves as God sees us, the object of infinite love and unremitting solicitude."[3] They whet our appetite for the Infinite. They suggest that the *kabōd Yahweh* must be defined as absolute love. They imply that our awe of God is limited by our impoverished imagination. They intimate that beyond all the words we use about God—*transcendence, kabōd divinity,* even *God*—lies a mysterious Reality that we cannot name. Thus, the mystic and theologian Meister Eckhart exclaimed, "I pray that I may be quit of God, that I may find God."

Rahner, one of the most important theologians of the twentieth century, declared that we need these artists and mystics to disrupt our complacency. "Eternal God, let them say what Your Spirit has given in their hearts," he prayed, "rather than that which would make pleasant hearing to those who represent the forces of all that is average."[4]

Fourteenth-century mystic Catherine of Siena is one of three women who have been honored by Catholic Christianity as Doctor of the Church, because of the depth of her writings on the spiritual life. She often began her prayers, "O Divine Madman." When this brilliant, fiery Italian woman was asked to describe the God of her journey, she whispered, "He is *pazzo d'amore, ebro d'amore*"—he is crazed with love, drunk with love.

To artists and mystics we must add the category of clowns—those who let God out of the box of our predetermined propriety. Clowns are instruments of grace, imploring in the voice of God, "Lighten up, ragamuffins!" Their somersaults, back-flips, and unpredictable high jinks tinker with our straitlaced logic, which alleges that ultimate significance can be found in the tangible, the visible, the perishable. Their spiritual direction to us follows the counsel of the psalmist: "Look up at the Lord with gladness and smile" (Ps. 40:16, NAB).

As we stare at their outlandish costumes, we recognize a lighthearted, whimsical stance toward life. As we respond to their offer of unaffected graciousness and sincere friendliness, our inflated sense of self-importance rushes out of us like air from a pinpricked balloon. They invite us to reclaim the child we once were, to suspend temporarily our mortal seriousness about the image we project to the world, the size of our waistline, the outcome of the Super Bowl. They giggle at my pathetic obsession with crafting this modest little book into a spiritual masterpiece. Amid the hurly-burly of Wall Street, the teeming traffic of rush hour, the long lines at the supermarket, their unexpected presence encourages us to reexamine our priorities, and does so with far greater effect than the apocalyptic threats of the doomsday preacher on the street corner.

Contemporaries of Francis of Assisi called him *le jongleur de Dieu*—the clown of God. At the first mass meeting of Franciscans, with three thousand brothers in attendance, Francis gently instructed the birds to stop chirping so that the friars might hear his sermon. They obeyed instantly. He tamed a wolf who was eating people in the village of Gubbio and extracted a promise from the locals to provide food each night for the carnivore. He picked up two stray pieces of wood, pretending that one was a bow and the other a fiddle, and sang love songs to God in French. He composed a canticle praising God for Brother Sun, Sister Moon, Brother Fire, Sister Water, and even Sister Death. He often stood on his head to see the world upside down, reminding his neighbors and himself that life on planet earth hangs precariously on the strings of God's loving-kindness.

This unlikely trio of artists, mystics, and clowns serves the ministry of the Word by expanding our understanding of the *kabōd Yahweh* through their original and startling insights; they deepen our trust by reminding us to submerge the enormous difficulty of suffering and evil in the borderless sea of infinite wisdom and absolute love; they force us to pose the question, "Is God different from what we perceive?" They lay bare an incandescent truth long concealed by ignorance, myopia, and inauthentic tradition: our perceptions of God, of our fellow ragamuffins, and of ourselves are flat-out wrong.

Why do campus ministers at Christian colleges and universities spend an inordinate amount of their time with incoming freshmen who abandoned God, church, and religious practice the moment they split from parental sanction? Why does the National Guild of Christian Psychiatrists report on the widespread phenomenon of clients tormented by intense feelings of guilt, shame, remorse, and self-punishment? Why does the melancholy spirit of Chekhov's plays—"You are living badly, my friend"—haunt the Christian conscience? Why is the local church often a dispirited assembly of brooding Hamlets and wiped-out Willie Lomans? Why do alcoholism, workaholism, and other addictive behaviors continue to increase within the faith community? Why, as writer John Kirvan asks, do we content ourselves with the shallow trivializing of our lives and dreams, with so much of what today passes for "spirituality"? Why do disciples of all ages race off to a Michael W. Smith concert with gleeful anticipation but shuffle off to Sunday service with the sacramental slump of the terminally ill?

Thirty-seven years of pastoral experience with Catholics, mainline Protestants, evangelicals, fundamentalists, Seventh Day Adventists, blacks, whites, Asians, and Hispanics tell me unmistakably that many a believer's perception of God is radically wrong.

In like fashion, our take on others becomes a simple act of reductionism. Bill Gates is a computer geek, Boy George a flamboyant gay, Rupert Murdoch a power-mad billionaire, Mother Teresa a saint, Bill Clinton a sinner, my boss a dork, my pastor a dweeb, the street person a bum, the waitress a function, Tiger Woods a phenomenon, Wolfgang Amadeus Mozart a brainy zany, Tony Campolo a radical preacher. Our perceptions are woefully inadequate.

In his Pulitzer Prize–winning novel *American Pastoral,* Philip Roth writes:

> You fight your superficiality, your shallowness, so as to try to come at people without unreal expectations, without an overload of bias or hope or arrogance, as untanklike as you can be. . . . You come at them unmenacingly on your own ten toes instead of

> tearing up the turf with your caterpillar treads, take them on with an open mind, as equals . . . and yet *you never fail to get them wrong* [italics added]. You might as well have the brain of tank. You get them wrong before you meet them, while you're anticipating meeting them; you get them wrong while you're with them; and then you go home to tell somebody else about the meeting and you get them all wrong again. Since the same generally goes for them with you, the whole thing is really a dazzling illusion empty of all perception, an astonishing farce of misperception . . . so ill-equipped are we all to envision another's interior workings and invisible aims.[5]

Wrong thinking about God and people often begins with a debased image of ourselves. As we continue to confuse our perception of ourselves with the mystery that we really are, self-rejection is inevitable. When a former student of mine at the University of Steubenville started her student teaching, she was rattled one day by an unexpected visit from her supervisor. Her class of second-graders suddenly became a gaggle of brash, screaming little monsters. The room was a war zone. Chaos reigned. Later, the sullen supervisor informed my student—at the time in her senior year—that she had no gift for teaching and should change her major immediately.

When Anne returned to campus humiliated, her roommate of three years was busy with homework and offered no greeting. Anne lambasted her roomie's insensitivity, blasted her as a fair-weather friend, and stormed out the door. Then she visited me to declare that she no longer believed in God and that trust in a compassionate Savior was ludicrous. Brutal criticism by a superior had savaged her self-worth. What ensued was predictable.

Send in the artists, mystics, and clowns. Their fertile imagination pours the new wine of the gospel into fresh wineskins (Luke 5:38). With fresh language, poetic vision, and striking symbols, they express God's inexpressible Word in artistic forms that are charged with the power of God, engaging our minds and stirring our hearts as they flare and flame.

"HEAVEN AND EARTH are full of your glory," cries the psalmist. The poet Gerard Manley Hopkins writes, "The world is charged with the grandeur of God." Thomas Plunkett insists, "I see His blood upon the rose." St. Augustine rhapsodizes, "O Beauty ever ancient, ever new."

In a country degraded by blighted neighborhoods and ravaged landscapes, the spiritual visionaries quiet our cultivated fears and inspire trust by lifting our eyes to the extravagant beauty of God manifested in creation. In his commentary on Psalm 148, Augustine asks, "Does God proclaim Himself in the wonders of creation?" He then answers, "No. All things proclaim Him, all things speak. Their beauty is the voice by which they announce God, by which they sing, 'It is you who made me beautiful, not me myself but you.'" The poets, singers, songwriters, novelists, musicians, clowns, and mystics enable the voices to creation to shout, "How beautiful is the One who made us!"

As a child, John Henry Newman imagined that behind every flower there lurked an angel who made it grow and blossom. Later in life, as the foremost theologian in England, he wrote, "The reality is more profound. It is God Himself who can be discovered in the beauty of sensible things."

Even Jesus marveled at the beauty surrounding him. "Look at the wildflowers. They never primp or shop, but have you ever seen color and design quite like it? The ten best-dressed men and women in the country look shabby alongside them" (Matt. 6:28–29, *The Message*).

Those who look beyond the literal see the world as a metaphor for God. When they direct us to the majesty of the mountains, the beauty of the prairies, the variety of wildflowers along the roadside, the smell of mint and hay on a summer morning, the rumble of a train through the valley, the sound of a waterfall, they birth the Word in our midst. They dare us to dream of our homeland, where eye has not seen, neither has ear heard, nor has the imagination conceived of the beauty that awaits us.

6

INFINITE AND INTIMATE

All human attempts to express the inexpressible—or, as philosopher Alan Watts put it, "to eff the ineffable"—remain woefully inadequate because of the huge quantitative and qualitative difference between our stumbling articulation and the divine Reality.

Kabōd is not a safe topic. It induces a feeling of terror before the Infinite and exposes as sham our empty religious talk and pointless activity, our idle curiosity and ludicrous pretensions of importance, our frantic busyness. The awareness that the eternal, transcendent God of Jesus Christ is our absolute future gives us the shakes. One day out of the blue comes the thought of our inevitable death, and the thought is so troubling that we want to live the rest of our lives in a shoe.

Small wonder that there is a deafening silence from our pulpits and publishers about the transcendent character of Almighty God. And who can blame us? Throughout the history of salvation God has revealed his presence but never his essence. Since the Holy One is ultimately unknowable, we can only stutter and stammer about an omnipotent deity who, with effortless ease, created a star 264 trillion miles away.

As a spiritual leader, I do not want to appear stupid. Nor do I want to sound like a blathering boob or a wimpy wuss. Given the very real danger of both options in the face of the unknowable, prudence dictates that I avoid the issue of God's transcendence altogether. Furthermore, I want the congregation to like me and to feel *good* about having spent an hour of their precious time in church on Sunday morning. Sending parishioners from the building quaking and trembling and needing to reexamine the entire direction of their lives, sending them off feeling that they are being stalked by an implacable God who demands nothing less than everything, would be not only an example of masochism but an act of professional suicide. I am not pastoring a Holy Roller assembly. Leave the shaking and quaking to the Shakers and Quakers, I say!

But we pay a price for steering clear of transcendence and unknowability. The loss of a sense of transcendence among today's believers has caused incalculable harm to Christian spirituality and to the interior life of individual Christians.

The first casualty has been silent reverence, radical amazement, and affectionate awe at the infinite goodness of God—those traits that are embodied in the scriptural term "fear of the Lord." Adoration, which flows naturally from the aptitude to appreciate the grandeur of divine reality, is conspicuously absent in our prayer life. Quiet time is often not quiet. Our designated prayer time is generally consumed by hurried meditation on a scripture passage, a run through the Rolodex of persons to intercede/petition for, and occasional expressions of gratitude for the gifts of our lives—faith, health, family, and friends. The inner urgency to fall prostrate before the Infinite rarely intrudes on our consciousness. Recent studies have shown that the average congregation on a Sunday morning can tolerate only fifteen seconds of silence before someone feels compelled to break it with an announcement, a song, a prophecy, or whatever.

Ironically, the church itself often impedes our efforts to reach inward and upward toward God. As Parker Palmer notes:

> Too often the church is an enemy of our solitude. Too often the church is one more agent in the vast social conspiracy of togetherness and noise aimed at distracting us from encountering ourselves. The church keeps us busy on this cause or that, this committee or that, trying to provide meaning through

> motion until we get "burned out" instead and withdraw from the church's life. Even in its core act of worship the church provides little space for the silent and solitary inward journey to occur (sometimes filling the available space with noisy exhortations to take that very journey!).[1]

When the glory of the transcendent God is not addressed, our focus shifts to human behavior, the cultivation of virtues and the extirpation of vices, the qualities of discipleship, and so on. Personal responsibility replaces personal response to God, and we become engrossed in our efforts to grow in holiness. Our primary concern becomes our spiritual, intellectual, and emotional well-being. When other Christians ask us if we are happy, we automatically respond in the affirmative or brush them off with a benevolent smile even if we are close to tears.

Obviously, there is something pokey and cramping about this inordinate attention devoted to ourselves, the state of our souls, and the presence or absence of happiness in our hearts. As Simon Tugwell notes, "One of the surest ways to avoid being happy is to insist on being happy at all costs. The religion of cheerfulness, as Father Brown reminds us, is a cruel religion, and maybe the best way not to go mad is not to mind too much if you do go mad."[2]

Moralizing surges to the fore in this unbalanced spirituality. At the very outset, it presents a warped idea of the relationship between God and humans. From her parents a child learns of a deity who strongly disapproves of disobedience, hitting one's brothers and sisters, and telling lies. When the little one goes to school, she realizes that God shares the fussy concerns of her teachers. At church, she learns that God has another set of priorities: she is told that he is displeased that the congregation is not growing numerically, that irregular attendance is the norm, and that his recurring fiscal demands are not being met.

When she reaches high school, she discovers that God's interests have expanded to an obsession with sex, drinking, and drugs. After twelve years of Christian indoctrination at home, school, and church, the teenager realizes with resentment that God has been used as a sanction by all those who have been responsible for her discipline—as when Mommy and Daddy, at their wits' end over her mischievous antics as a toddler, alluded to "the eternal spanking." Through this indoctrination, God is unwittingly associated with fear in most young hearts.[3]

Moralism and its stepchild, legalism, pervert the character of the Christian life. By the time young people enter college, they have often abandoned God, church, and religion. If they persevere in religious practices, their need to appease an arbitrary God turns Sunday worship into a superstitious insurance policy designed to protect the believer against God's whims. When wounded people fail, as inevitably they must, they engage in denial to protect themselves from punishment. The perfect image must be protected at all costs.

We work hard to protect our collective image as well. When a youth worker at a church in a midwestern town dared to confess to the staff one morning that he struggled with pornography, he received his letter of termination that afternoon.

Clearly, the God of our imagination is not worthy of trust, adoration, praise, reverence, or gratitude. And yet, if we are unwilling to address the issue of transcendence, that is the only deity we know.

The loss of transcendence has left in its wake the flotsam of distrustful, cynical Christians, angry at a capricious God, and the jetsam of smug bibliolatrists who claim to know precisely what God is thinking and exactly what he plans to do.

A CAVEAT is necessary at this juncture—one that leads to the final point of this chapter: transcendence must be conjoined with immanence; heaven must be balanced with earth. In other words, God's distance must be complemented by his nearness.

An exclusive emphasis on the divine *kabōd* and the transcendent mystery of God banishes God from our world and our lives. He remains far away, aloof in his infinite majesty. He dwells in unapproachable light. The whole universe is too small to contain his immensity. We can no more catch a hurricane in a shrimp net or Niagara Falls in a coffee cup than we can grasp the infinity of God's reality. A one-sided focus on his Otherness reduces the Holy One to a cosmic observer, a distant outsider disengaged from the yaw and pitch of the human struggle.

Immanence is not the *opposite* of transcendence but its *correlative*; immanence and transcendence are two sides of the same coin, two facets of the same divine reality. Transcendence means that God cannot be confined to the world, that he is never this rather than that, here rather then there. Immanence, on the other hand, means that God is *wholly* involved with us, "that he is living in all that is as its innermost mystery,"[4] that he is here in his mysterious nearness. (More on this in the next chapter.) Disregard of God's immanence deprives us of any sense of intimate belonging, while inattention to his transcendence robs God of his godliness.

In the pages of church history we find a luminous illustration of the devastating consequences wrought by unbalanced attention to one or the other aspect of the Godhead. It started with the greatest of all the ancient heresies, Arianism, which denied the divinity of Christ. The issue was momentous: if Jesus was not divine, he was just another batch of chemicals to decay in a tomb provided by Joseph of Arimathea, and hope died on Calvary.

The church reacted with a one-sided emphasis on Christ's divinity at the expense of his humanity. It was not a question of orthodoxy, as Godfrey Diekmann has noted, but rather of seeing certain truths out of focus,[5] as when a camera is sharply focused on a single rhododendron and the adjacent flowers get blurred.

The long-range effects of this distortion introduced a spiritual malaise that was to last for centuries. First and most important, Jesus the God-man had crossed over, so to speak, and was now on God's side. Christ himself was not "our brother in the flesh", but the awful and unapproachable God. As his humanity receded into the background, Jesus was relegated to the infinite sphere of the Divine. Jesus' intimate communion with his disciples was obscured. His word, "Make your home in me, as I make mine in you" (John 15:4), was ignored or forgotten. As the Vine was severed from the branches, the Christ of God became remote and inaccessible. The memory of Jesus as "a man like us in all things but sin" (Heb. 4:15) was overlaid by his divine presence. Who would dare to approach our elder Brother with the "confidence that we would find mercy and grace in time of need?" (4:16).

The skewed stress on the divinity of Christ in this christological heresy inevitably opened up a yawning gulf between the children of God and the transcendent Savior. How did this affect the participation of the laity in their life of communal worship?

The anti-Arian reaction, stressing transcendence over immanence and Christ's divinity above his humanity, turned the eucharistic celebration of the people of God into a strictly clerical affair. The high priesthood of Jesus Christ was not exercised through the "royal priesthood" (1 Pet. 2:9) of the laity but only through the ordained minister. The Communion rail was introduced to separate the sanctuary from the nave in order to safeguard the Holy of Holies from defilement by the wretched laity, and the altar was turned around so that the priest's back was to the people. Kneeling replaced standing during the liturgical prayer of the canon, breast-beating accompanied various prayers, the genuflection was introduced during the recitation of the creed, and the taking of Communion—preceded by a new prayer, "Lord, I am not worthy to receive you . . . " (who can gainsay that?)—declined precipitously.

Participation in the Eucharist deteriorated into mere attendance. Jesus, seen as the divine Consecrator, was viewed primarily as God. Thus, the bowing of the head and the beating of the breast at the words of consecration, *"Hoc est enim corpus meum"* ("This is my body"), became the standard posture. In fact, many of the faithful raced from one mass to another on Sunday morning, ignoring the liturgy of the Word just to be present for the consecration; and with the repetition of *"Hoc est enim corpus meum,"* the phrase "hocus-pocus," used derisively by cynics, entered our vocabulary.[6]

The towering importance of the above caveat—that transcendence must be conjoined with immanence, that divinity must be coupled with humanity, that heaven must be balanced with earth, and that God's distance must be complemented by his nearness—is essential if we are to grasp the true meaning of the glory of Jesus.

7 

TRUSTING JESUS

Faith arises from the personal experience of Jesus as Lord.

Hope is reliance on the promise of Jesus, accompanied by the expectation of fulfillment.

Trust is the winsome wedding of faith and hope.

In Luke's Gospel, the centurion professes his faith in Jesus with the words, "Sir, I am not worthy to have you under my roof," and hope in his promise, "but give the word and let my servant be healed" (7:7). Then, "taken aback, Jesus address[es] the accompanying crowd: 'I've yet to come across this kind of simple trust anywhere in Israel'" (7:9, *The Message*).

Faith + hope = trust.

In John's Gospel, a royal official with a sick son comes to Jesus. "Sir," he pleads, "come down before my child dies." Jesus tells him, "Return home. Your son will live" (4:49–50, NAB). The man puts his trust in the words Jesus has spoken to him and starts for home. Once again, faith in the person of Jesus and hope in his promise.

In Mark, a father brings to Jesus his son possessed by a mute spirit. "If out of the kindness of your heart you can do anything to help us, please do!" he pleads. Jesus says, "If you can? Everything is possible to a man who trusts." The boy's father immediately exclaims, "I do believe! Help my lack of trust" (9:22–24, NAB). What is missing here? Hope. The boy's father believes in Jesus but lacks conviction that his expectation for healing will be fulfilled.

Faith and hope work together to form a trusting disciple.

In his farewell discourse Jesus says, "Eternal life is this: *to know you,* the only true God, and Jesus Christ whom you have sent" (John 17:3).

Here is a point of capital importance for our biblical understanding of trusting Jesus. In Western thinking knowledge is the intellectual apprehension of reality, the mind's affirmation of a truth perceived. In the Hebrew and Christian scriptures, knowledge is *felt;* it arises from an *experience* of God in faith and love rather than from human investigation.[1] Knowledge is the fruit of a faith-encounter with Jesus as the Christ. It is simply not possible to receive the revelation of God in the transcendent/immanent Christ without experience. Experience is an essential part of knowing Jesus and of the whole concept of revelation. As Dutch theologian Edward Schillebeeckx asserts, "Christianity is not a message which has to be believed, but an experience of faith that becomes a message."[2]

Before discussing the nature of that experience, it must be noted that Jesus alone reveals who God is. He is the source of our information about transcendence/divinity. We cannot deduce anything about Jesus from what we think we know about God; however, we must deduce everything about God from what we know about Jesus.[3] This implies that all of our prevailing images and understandings of God must crumble in the earthquake of Jesus' self-disclosure. Trust means the willingness to become absolutely empty of all terrifying and comforting images of God that we have held, so that the gift of God in Jesus Christ may come to us on God's terms.

If we do not allow Jesus to change our image of God, then we cannot profess him, as the apostle Thomas did, as "my Lord and my God." Much as we would like to, we cannot confine the humble, compassionate Carpenter within our mental limitations, thereby robbing him of his Otherness. No matter how much he is like us, no matter how many attitudes, values, and human characteristics we share in common, Jesus is also altogether different from us. In the depth of his personality he is divine, totally Other, and the *kabōd Yahweh* rests upon him. Jesus remains as mysterious in his nearness as he is in his transcendence. For me and many others, Jesus is the revelation of the only God worthy of trust.

The full experience of Jesus is an encounter with him on both the divine and the human levels of existence, since he belongs to both. This experience—this moment of recognition, if you will—is not reserved to a privileged few but is graciously granted to the high and the low, the rich and the poor, the educated and the illiterate—in short, to anyone seriously seeking the God of Jesus. (It must be stated, however, that to seek the experience simply for the sake of experience is to seek self, not God.)

The experience of Jesus as Lord, which brings forth the response of faith, varies as widely as the people who encounter it. It spans Paul's *kabōd* experience on the road to Damascus, and a woman's quiet, transforming experience during a powerful proclamation of the Word, and the rescue from hopeless defeat experienced by alcoholic Bill Wilson (co-founder of Alcoholics Anonymous) in a hospital room in New York City. Whatever the circumstances, the same thread is woven into each experience. Let scripture scholar John McKenzie explain:

> The basic element seems to be recognition. We recognize that the person whom we have encountered speaks to our innermost being, supplies our needs, satisfies our desires. We recognize that this person gives life meaning. I do not say a new meaning, but meaning simply, for we realize that before we

> encountered this person life had no real meaning. We recognize that this person has revealed to us not only himself but our own true self as well. We recognize that we cannot be our own true self except by union with this person. In him the obscure is illuminated, the uncertain yields to the certain, insecurity is replaced by a deep sense of security. In him we find we have achieved an understanding of many things which baffled us. We recognize in his person strength and power which we can sense passing from him to us. Most certainly if most obscurely, we recognize that in this person we have encountered God; and that we shall not encounter God in any other way.[4]

Faith, born of this indispensable experience, infuses the felt knowledge of "the only true God, and Jesus Christ whom [God has] sent." The quiet certitude of the believer translates simply as, "I know that I know that I know," however dimly and through a glass darkly.

Eighteen hundred years after the call of Abraham, God made his infinite word finite. At last we are spared the feeling of terror before the Infinite. God has come to us in a human word, and his name is Jesus Christ. The *kabōd Yahweh*, which frightens us out of all sense of security, speaks to us in human language, and the word *love* is no longer anything we must fear. When Jesus says, "As the Father has loved me, so I have loved you. Live on in my love" (John 15:9), this word comes from a human heart. While his love is incomparably greater than our human love, because his heart is the heart of God, it is still love and becomes in a limited way comprehensible to our feeble understanding.

The *kabōd* shines on the face of Jesus, and the absolute glory of God is manifest as the sheer glory of love. Since the incarnation, the question is no longer *Is Jesus God-like?* but *Is God Jesus-like?* The transcendent/immanent God is, in the classic phrase of St. Augustine, "more intimate than my deepest self and higher than my utmost peak."[5] In the person of Jesus, God is nearer to me than I am to myself. Underlying the messianic titles of Savior, Redeemer, and so on is the staggering truth that Jesus "bodies forth" the infinite love of God. Thus Bernard Lonergan insists, "Every authentic spiritual experience is an experience of unrestricted, unconditional being in love."[6]

If the night is bad and our nerves are shattered and darkness comes and pain is all around and the Holy One is conspicuous by his absence and we want to know the true feelings of the inscrutable God toward us, we must turn and look at Jesus. This path to God is reflected in Karl Rahner's prayer:

> Grant, O Infinite God, that I may ever cling fast to Jesus Christ, my Lord. Let his heart reveal to me how you are disposed toward me. I shall look upon his

> heart when I desire to know who you are. The eye of my mind is blinded whenever it looks only at your Infinity, in which you are totally present in each and every aspect at once. Then I am surrounded by the darkness of your unboundedness, which is harsher than all my earthly night. But instead I shall gaze upon his human heart, O God of our Lord Jesus Christ, and then I shall be sure that you love me.[7]

If someone were to ask you, "What is the one thing in life that is certain?" you would have to answer, "The love of Christ." Not parents, not family, not friends. Not art or science or philosophy or any of the products of human wisdom. Only the love of Christ. You could not even say "God's love," because the truth that God is love is ultimately known only through Jesus Christ. Such is the certitude of faith rising from lived experience. I know that I know that I know. Therefore, it is fitting that all our prayers, both public and private, end with "through Christ our Lord."

Our trust in Jesus grows as we shift from making self-conscious efforts to be good to allowing ourselves to be loved as we are (not as we should be). The Holy Spirit moves us from the head to the heart, from intellectual cognition to experiential awareness. An inward stillness pervades our being, and the time of prayer is characterized by less rational reflection and speaking and more contemplative quiet and listening.

Self-absorption fades into self-forgetfulness, as we fix our gaze on the brightness of the Lord. In the words of Paul, "We are transfigured much like the Messiah, our lives gradually becoming brighter and more beautiful as God enters our lives and we become like him" (2 Cor. 3:18, *The Message*).

Jesus, the Light of the world, is the visible manifestation of the *kabōd Yahweh,* the infinite glory of God. The synoptic writers, eager to establish this truth from the outset, tell of the glory of God which illuminated the shepherds at Bethlehem as a dazzling light (Luke 2:9). Jesus shares the luminous brilliance of his Father, and this will be revealed in his Second Coming as judge (Matt. 16:29, Mark 8:38, Luke 21:27). The radiance of the glory of Jesus is manifested by anticipation in his transfiguration (Luke 9:31f).

John asserts that the disciples saw his glory through his display of thaumaturgic power at the wedding feast of Cana. "This was the first of the signs given by Jesus; it was given at Cana in Galilee. He let his glory be seen, and the disciples believed in him" (2:11). In the Johannine writings especially, Jesus is glorified through his passion, death, and resurrection.

Other New Testament writers also discuss *kabōd* issues. In the Letter to the Hebrews, Jesus is spoken of as the reflection of the glory of the Father (1:3). In First Corinthians and again in the Letter of James (2:1), Jesus is given the title "Lord of glory" (2:8).

Countless scriptural examples testify to the early Christian community's perception of Jesus as Lord of glory; there is no need to belabor them. The post-Easter proclamation of the gospel verifies Søren Kierkegaard's comment, "Life is lived forward but understood backward."[8] After the resurrection, the assembly of believers intensely reexamined the Hebrew scriptures and saw the *kabōd Yahweh* manifested in the unique event when God himself assumed our human nature in the person of Jesus.

Why belabor this point? Why go to such lengths to make strikingly obvious what is obviously striking?

Because the personal experience of the glory of Jesus, the shattering encounter with the transcendent/immanent Christ, is the foundation of the faith and the hope that form and inform a life of naked trust.

Jesus assured us of two things: presence and promise. It is not tautologous to say *the promise of his presence* ("I'll be with you every day of your life until your time runs out") and *the presence of his promise* (Christ in you *now* and your hope of glory *down the road*). Jesus never guaranteed that we would be spared suffering or victimization by evil-doing; in fact, he said flatly, "In the world you will have trouble" (John 16:33). What he promised was that during our desolate hours there would be one set of footprints. In varying degrees, suffering and loss touch every life—as does the presence of God in Christ if we have faith in his presence and hope in his promise.

In the midst of the ruins—in the premature death of a

loved one, in the hell on earth we call a crack house, in the ache of heartbreak, in the sheer malevolence of Kosovo and Rwanda—the presence of God abides. The trusting disciple, often through clenched teeth, says, in effect, God is still trustworthy, but not because of unrestricted power to intervene on my behalf; he is trustworthy because of a promise given and sustained in Christian communities throughout generations.[9]

In the midst of tragic events that leave us bereft of understanding, trust does not demand explanations but turns to the One who promised, "I will not leave you orphans" (John 14:18). In the face of a pressing need for answers and solutions to life's problems—answers that are not quickly forthcoming—trust in the Wisdom and Power who is Jesus Christ knows how to wait.

Dennis Rainey tells the story of a missionary family home on furlough, staying at the lake house of a friend. On the day in question, Dad was puttering in the boathouse, Mom in the kitchen, and the three children, ages four, seven, and twelve, were on the lawn. Four-year-old Billy escaped his oldest sister's watchful eye and wandered down to the wooden dock. The shiny aluminum boat caught his eye, but unsteady feet landed him in eight-foot-deep water.

When the twelve-year-old screamed, Dad came running out. Realizing what had happened, he dove into the murky depths. Frantically he felt for his son, but twice, out of breath, he had to return to the surface.

Filling his lungs once more, he dove down and found Billy clinging to a wooden pier several feet under. Prying the boy's fingers loose, he bolted to the surface with Billy in his arms.

Safely ashore, his father asked, "Billy, what were you doing down there?" The little one replied, "Just waitin' on you, Dad, just waitin' on you."

Young as he was, the boy no doubt had a history with his father—a history of feeling safe, protected, accepted, and loved. He knew from experience that his father delighted in him. Naturally the boy had a healthy, positive self-image: he had come to know that he was loved, and he had felt knowledge of his father's faithfulness. Cooler heads might judge the boy presumptuous and assert that he had showed reckless disregard for his safety. He should have taken *control* of his desperate situation, they would say. And surely there is a measure of truth here. However, when taking control becomes our *routine* response to troubled relationships and worrisome problems, God is not our co-pilot; he's not even aboard.

Like faith and hope, trust cannot be self-generated. I cannot simply *will* myself to trust. What outrageous irony: the one thing that I am responsible for throughout my life I cannot generate. The one thing I *need* to do I *cannot* do. But such is the meaning of radical dependence. It consists in theological virtues, in divinely ordained gifts. Why reproach myself for my lack of trust? Why waste time beating myself up for something I cannot affect?

What *does* lie within my power is paying attention to the faithfulness of Jesus. That's what I am asked to do: pay attention to Jesus throughout my journey, remembering his kindnesses (Ps. 103:2).

My first publisher told me the story of a summer afternoon when he was driving along the New Jersey Turnpike. One hundred yards ahead in the same lane was a Lincoln Town Car. Tom was shocked when he saw the right rear door of the Lincoln, still moving at full speed, swing open. The passenger threw a collie onto the pavement. The dog hit the concrete and rolled into a ditch. Bleeding profusely, the collie got up and started to run after the car and the owner who had cruelly abandoned him. His relentless faithfulness was not conditioned or diminished by the abuse and callous disregard of his master.

The dogged fidelity of Jesus in the face of our indifference to his affection and our rampant ingratitude for his faithfulness—he is *always* faithful, for he cannot disown his own self (2 Tim. 2:11)—is a mystery of such mind-bending magnitude that the intellect buckles and theology bows in its presence. Humbly acknowledging our limitations, we are driven to the fervent prayer, "Lord, I do believe! Help my lack of trust."

Woody Allen wryly remarked that ninety percent of life is just showing up. To trust someone is a gut feeling that he will show up in fair weather and foul, in good times and bad, in the yaw and pitch of the human struggle.

Trusting someone does not imply that we have tested that person out thoroughly, proved infallibly that she is trustworthy. Our trust is based not on proof but on an intuitive sense, an instinct, a feeling—a feeling not without some basis, of course, but likewise not the end result of a syllogism or a questionnaire. Trust comes from some experience of the other person, an experience not reducible to proof. Most often, it grows up in a relationship of mutual love, one in which we have loved, and been loved by, the other.

A fine example of trust can be seen in the literary masterpiece of the Wisdom movement, the Book of Job. Though Job is beset by suffering and loss on every side, his trust endures even when understanding fails. The scriptural document does not present his experience as a way to understand evil but as a way to live with it. The story of Job implicitly states that we can endure the unwanted intrusion of evil when we have experienced a theophany—that is, an insight into the reality of God.

Walter Burghardt writes: "Only trust makes evil endurable—trust not because God has offered proof, but because God has shown his face. The movement in summary: from experience of God to love of God to trust in God."[10]

The ragged journey of this vagabond evangelist has brought me in contact with a multitude of people. When

I preach the gospel, I do not feel like a confident, conquering apostle who radiates superhuman strength and unshakable inner security. Addressing professional youth workers or seasoned, sage elders who have listened to speakers far more gifted, I have the tormenting feeling of being "sounding brass and tinkling cymbal." As my friend Paul Sheldon will testify, I am amazed without fail (even after twenty-five years of doing this stuff full-time) when people receive my ministry gratefully and invite me to return. I continue to marvel at the many people who have allowed me to enter the inner chamber of their hearts because they have been able to recognize Jesus hidden in me. And I shake my head in grateful surprise at the miracle of his grace at work in my ministry.

Then I return to the motel, pack my bag, and go on to the next place. Along the highway I meet others who are companions for a time, since we are going in the same direction. When one of us takes an exit, without a word or a wave of farewell, we part company, never to see one another again. It is not a cause for grief or self-pity, but simply the nature of the itinerant lifestyle. At times, however, in some rare and gratuitous moment on the road, I meet someone and experience what can only be described as a moment of mutual recognition. With the passing of time, I develop a friendship with that person, and our desire to spend time together grows. When ministry calls me to return to that friend's hometown or city, it would be unthinkable not to have dinner with him.

Such a friend allows me to be myself, thoughtful one moment and silly the next. Between us, trust grows. If a word of fraternal correction is needed, the friend offers it directly, but the pained expression on his face tells me how difficult the reproof is for him. And yet he has the courage to tell me something unpleasant but necessary—something that others should tell me but do not. (They renege for fear that I will not like them anymore. Their emotional equilibrium is more important to them than my spiritual growth.) With each interaction, trust of my friend grows deeper.

Paul and a few others have stood with me throughout the bad weather of life. I thought of them immediately when I read this passage from Frederick Buechner's novel *Brendan*.

> Pushing down hard with his fists on the table top he heaved himself up to where he was standing. For the first time we saw he wanted one leg. It was gone from the knee joint down. He was hopping sideways to reach for his stick in the corner when he lost his balance. He would have fallen in a heap if Brendan hadn't leapt forward and caught him.
>
> "I'm as crippled as the dark world," Gildas said.
>
> "If it comes to that, which one of us isn't, my dear?" Brendan said.
>
> Gildas with but one leg. Brendan sure he'd misspent his whole life entirely. Me that had left my

wife to follow him and buried our only boy. The truth of what Brendan said stopped all our mouths. We was cripples all of us. For a moment or two there was no sound but the bees.

"To lend each other a hand when we're falling," Brendan said. "Perhaps that's the only work that matters in the end."[11]

In my efforts to overcome my lifelong struggle with self-hatred, the despair of ever being worthy of love, I have been aided immeasurably by trusted and trusting friends who, with no ulterior motive, see something in me that I cannot see in myself. They do not merely *tell* me; they relate to me in a way which *shows* that they find me lovable. Learning to trust my friends has been a slow but invaluable process.

Honesty with others and with self is a precious commodity seldom found in either the world at large or the church. To disclose our dark secrets to another is a risky business. There may be reprisals, as the midwestern youth worker I mentioned in the previous chapter learned at great cost. We all wrestle with the question I posed in *Abba's Child*:

> Is there anyone I can level with? Anyone I dare tell that I am benevolent and malevolent, chaste and randy, compassionate and vindictive, selfless and selfish, that beneath my brave words lives a frightened

> child, that I dabble in religion and pornography, that I have blackened a friend's character, betrayed a trust, violated a confidence, that I am tolerant and thoughtful, a bigot and a blowhard, that I hate hard rock?[12]

Sensing that if I bare my soul, I will be abandoned by my friends and ridiculed by my enemies, I remain in hiding, borrowing from the cosmetic kit to put on my pretty face. I veil my unstated distrust behind a cheerful countenance, mask my fears behind sanguine pretense, and present a false self that is mostly admirable, mildly prepossessing, and superficially happy. Later, I hate myself for my flagrant dishonesty.

Who can I turn to?

In what may be the most stunning sentence in the entire Bible, Jesus says, "I call you my friend" (John 15:15).

Commenting on these words, St. Augustine writes, "A friend is someone who knows everything about you and totally accepts you as you are."[13] Is this not the dream that we all share? Someday, somewhere, I am going to meet that person who really understands me—understands the words I speak and even the words I leave unspoken. The gospel proclaims that Jesus of Nazareth is the fulfillment of that dream. Paul Tillich's definition of trust remains the most meaningful of all to me. He defines trust as "the courage to accept acceptance."[14]

Raw honesty with Jesus about our doubts and anxieties, our lust and laziness, our shabby prayer life and stale religiosity, our mixed motives and divided hearts is the risk we take in the certainty of being acceptable and accepted. It is the full and mature expression of invincible trust. Jesus is the friend who will never fail, the faithful one who will never be lacking in fidelity, even when people are unfaithful to him, the stranger to self-hatred who estranges us from self-hatred.

German theologian Walter Kasper, after noting that personal experience is the sine qua non of biblical faith, concludes, "Experiencing God's love in Jesus Christ means experiencing that one has been unreservedly accepted, approved and *infinitely* loved [italics mine], that one can and should accept oneself and one's neighbor."[15]

Trust, grounded in faith and hope, reaches an unprecedented level in the experience of infinite love. It is useless to protest that such a concept is too big for us. Of *course* it is too big for us. The *kabōd Yahweh,* the absolute glory of God, is revealed in Jesus as absolute love, and we can only be brushed by it. Nevertheless, we are made for that which is too big for us. We are made for God, and nothing less will ever satisfy us.

Simon Tugwell writes, "We must allow our appetite for infinity to dislodge us whenever we are inclined to settle down and call it a day."[16] Hungering and thirsting for *more* disturbs complacency, induces a blessed state of disquiet, and propels our unending exploration into the mystery of God in Christ Jesus. Accepting no substitutes for what we really want leads to simplicity of life.

Methinks it is best to start adopting that stance right away, since the day will inevitably come when we shall have to surrender ourselves without any inhibition to the overwhelming attractiveness of Jesus.

Whether we be novices beginning the journey or veterans so close to the end of it that we never buy green bananas, whether we be spiritual giants or midgets, the response Jesus seeks is always the same: trust. In John's First Letter we read: "We ourselves have known and put our trust in God's love towards ourselves" (4:16). Or, in Eugene Peterson's felicitous translation, "We know it so well, we've embraced it heart and soul, this love that comes from God" *(The Message)*.

If we do not allow Jesus to change our perception of God, if we continue to cling to our pre-Christian images and distorted projections, if we think that Jesus is not easy to get on with (is touchy, unapproachable, easily annoyed or offended), we reject the gift of his friendship, disdain the open, airy, spacious atmosphere of his Kingdom, and opt for the dark and dreary dungeon of distrust.

But what about doubts and worries? Do they, too, signal a rejection of God's Kingdom?

Not necessarily. There can be no faith without doubt, no hope without anxiety, and no trust without worry. These shadow us from dawn to dusk; indeed, they appear even in our dreams. As long as we withhold internal *consent* to these varied faces of fear, they are no cause for alarm, because they are not voluntary. When they threaten to consume us, we can overpower them with a simple and deliberate act of trust: "Jesus, by your grace I grow still for a moment and I hear you say, 'Courage! It's me! Don't be afraid.' I place my trust in your presence and your love. Thank you."

Let us never underestimate the power of truth unleashed in our experience of Jesus and magnified in our fidelity to seeking his face. In his last days, Thomas Merton wrote in his *Asian Journal* that trust increases through our fidelity to the search and leads to "a certitude which is very, very deep because it is not our own personal certitude, it is the certitude of God Himself in us."[17]

After the initial experience, perseverance in the lifelong quest for greater intimacy with Jesus, no matter how often we stumble and fall, is not only the antidote to hopelessness and despair; it is the sure path to divine certitude that overcomes all doubts, anxieties, and worries. According to the fifteenth-century mystic Julian of Norwich, whom Merton considered one of England's two greatest theologians (along with John Henry Newman):

> It is God's will that we receive three things from him as gifts as we seek. The first is that we seek willingly and diligently without sloth, as that may be with his

> grace, joyfully and happily, without unreasonable depression and useless sorrow. The second is that we wait for him steadfastly, out of love for him, without grumbling and contending against him. . . . The third is that we have great trust in him, out of complete and true faith, for it is his will that we know that he will appear, suddenly and blessedly, to all his lovers.[18]

The experiential quality of faith and hope brings profound depth and dimension to the Abba relationship. From the available testimony (Mark 14:36), it seems that Jesus constantly addressed God as "Abba," an intimate, colloquial word meaning "Daddy" in the Aramaic. The label must have struck Jesus' contemporaries as irreverent and offensively familiar. But familiarity does not exclude respect. Reverence and the readiness to obey form the basis of Jesus' understanding of his Father. His extraordinary use of the affectionate form of address implies that we may approach God securely and confidently, as a little child would approach a loving father.

To pray "O almighty, eternal, infinite Abba" not only avoids mere sentimentality; it speaks to what I believe is the most important and urgent requirement of our generation—a new awareness of *transcendence*. Such an awareness in no way diminishes the warmth and tenderness of the label "Abba." To address God in this way is the boldest and simplest expression of the absolute trust that God is good, that he is on our side, "that as tenderly as a father treats his children, so Yahweh treats those who fear him" (Ps. 103:13).

The awareness of transcendence restores reverence, wonder, awe, and adoration to the "Abba, I belong to you" prayer. It is the Christian complement to the lapidary statement found in the Hasidic tradition: "Fear without love is an imperfection; love without fear is nothing at all."

The Letter to the Hebrews describes the efficacy of Jesus' prayer to his Abba: "He offered prayers and supplications with loud cries and tears to God . . . and he was heard because of his reverence" (5:7–8). I want neither a terrorist spirituality that keeps me in a perpetual state of fright about being in right relationship with my heavenly Father nor a sappy spirituality that portrays God as such a benign teddy bear that there is no aberrant behavior or desire of mine that he will not condone. I want a relationship with the Abba of Jesus, who is infinitely compassionate with my brokenness and at the same time an awesome, incomprehensible, and unwieldy Mystery.

When Jesus said, "Be compassionate as your Father is compassionate" (Luke 6:36), he intended that we should show compassion toward our neurotic selves and our neurotic neighbors. (Each morning I dialogue with my neuroses and inquire whether they are in a state of acute agitation or in their normal debilitating state. If the former, I ask for the grace to draw upon deeper reserves of empathy; if the latter, I rely on my regular reservoir of compassion. Later in the day, this helps me to be gentle with the nuttiness of my neighbors.)

This command of Jesus is also an invitation to deeper exploration into the *kabōd Yahweh*. While many of the psalms speak of *kabōd* as an overpowering force and a shattering reality, they also speak of shelter and protection for those who confide in Yahweh (Ps. 11, 16, 36). The forthright, candid, no-nonsense Nazarene carpenter takes us immeasurably beyond the Old Testament revelation, stating that the glory of God shows forth in an affection unbounded, a love unrestrained, and a compassion unconfined by our limited human experience.

Jesus says, in effect, Don't ever be so foolish as to measure my Father's compassion with your compassion. Don't ever be so silly as to compare your thin, pallid, wavering, capricious human compassion with mine, for I am God as well as man.

The great Franciscan theologian Duns Scotus maintained that if Adam and Eve had not sinned (and thus the human race had had no need of a Savior), Jesus would still have come to us as the revealer of the Father's compassion. He scandalized the religious establishment of first-century Palestine by his easy rapport with notorious sinners. Well, as the French are wont to say, "Plus ca change, plus c'est la même chose"—the more a thing changes, the more it is the same. The least we preachers could do is to speak with diffidence of infinite compassion.

Recovering the awareness of transcendence does not ostracize Abba from our human experience. He is not infinitely remote in his tremendous majesty. Paradoxically, as we enter the "cloud of unknowing" and all our cherished images of God are stripped away, Abba draws near to us in his Son, Jesus. "He who sees me sees the Father" (John 14:9). Jesus is the human face of God with all the same attitudes, attributes, and characteristics of his Abba. Paternal love is revealed in the fraternal love of Jesus, our Brother. "I do not say that I shall pray to the Father for you, because the Father himself loves you for loving me" (John 16:26–27). In order to have any understanding of Abba—not of his essence, which remains unknowable, but of his character—we must look to Jesus. Once again, to acknowledge Jesus as Lord is to make him the source of our information about divinity and to refuse to superimpose upon him our own ideas of divinity.

In 1968, on a wintry night brilliant with starshine, I stood on the edge of darkness awaiting the sunrise. The Spanish desert sands gleamed like silvered sugar. Over and over the wind whispered his name to me, "Abba, Abba." Neither thunderbolts nor flashes of lightning—simply a quiet, transforming experience. The all-night prayer vigil had ended, and something brand-new had begun. In a solitary cave in the Zaragosa wilderness, I was graced with the *felt knowledge* of the Father as my Abba. I was a child again, lost in wonder, adoration, and thanksgiving.

The experience of being the beloved child of the almighty, eternal, infinite Abba introduces a sense of "holy awe" to the cry, "Abba, I belong to you." The great psychic enslavement of fear gradually recedes when confronted with the greatness of God's love and compassion. Questions, speculations, and complaints at the absurdity of life, the random accidents and illnesses, the dark nights of the soul, the diminishment of our faculties through aging, our inevitable death, and even the last rag we cling to—our unimpeachable integrity and innocence—all seem inappropriate in the presence of infinite Goodness. Trust escalates "not because God has offered proof, but because God has shown his face," to again quote Walter Burghardt.

Why did John Lennon prove to be a false prophet when, in 1960, he predicted that in ten years the Beatles would be more popular than Jesus Christ? Dallas Willard provides an answer in his luminous work *The Divine Conspiracy*:

> I think we finally have to say that Jesus' enduring relevance is based on his historically proven ability to speak to, to heal and empower, the individual human condition. He matters because of what he brought

> and what he still brings to ordinary human beings, living their ordinary lives and coping daily with their surroundings. He promises wholeness for their lives. In sharing our weakness he gives us strength and imparts through his companionship a life that has the quality of eternity.[19]

In the final analysis, trusting Jesus comes down to obedience to his command, "Trust in God, and trust in me" (John 14:1).

8 

TAINTED TRUST

God instructs Moses: "Send men to reconnoiter the land of Canaan, which I am giving the Israelites" (Num. 13:1). The recon team spends forty days in stealthy exploration. They return to camp with good news and bad news. It's a land flowing with milk and honey, they say (still salivating over the exotic fruits they sampled), but a fierce street-gang who call themselves the *Anakim* roam the neighborhood. They are as huge as NFL linemen (no mention of tattoos or pierced noses and navels)—so big that the recon team feel like grasshoppers in their presence.

Fearless Caleb speaks up and says, "Let's go wipe 'em out and seize the territory!" His intimidated cohorts protest, "No way! They'll have us for breakfast." The Israelite community vacillates, then starts weeping and wailing. The people have terrifying nightmares once they put their heads on their pillows.

They believe in God. They have faith in Yahweh, and yet—because of fear of the *Anakim*—they abandon hope in his promise that they will take possession of Canaan. With the exception of Moses, Aaron, and Caleb, despair contaminates the Chosen People. Confronted with stronger battalions, faced with apparently insuperable obstacles, they allow their trust in Yahweh's guidance and protection to collapse. But faith in God without hope in his promises is tainted trust.

How well we know the Israelites' conundrum. Hesitation and uncertainty prevail. The craving for tangible reassurance of God's faithfulness increases. We press for more convincing proofs of abiding, divine presence. When they are not forthcoming, we decide to take control. Safety is our only passion. In a spiritual life charged with ambiguity, we cannot afford to make mistakes. Endless analysis replaces creative action. The willingness to risk is submerged in a raging sea of nagging doubts. We must have absolute clarity before we can proceed.

What we have failed to learn is that clarity, reassurance, and proof cannot create trust, sustain it, or guarantee any certainty of its presence.

Edward Farrell, author of *Prayer Is a Hunger,* maintains that the three greatest obstacles to trust are amnesia, inertia, and *mañana*. We are all subject to forgetfulness of

God's faithfulness in the past, laziness to act on the divine promise, and postponing until tomorrow what Jesus is asking of us today: childlike abandonment in trust.

When I entered the Franciscan Order in 1956, I was asked if I intended to be a candidate for the priesthood or for the brotherhood. I replied that I had not known I had a choice, and further I did not understand the difference between the two. I was informed that the brothers performed manual labor and were trained as cooks, cobblers, maintenance men, and so on. The priests were trained and ordained to preach the gospel and to celebrate the sacraments. Shy, introverted, and truly frightened by the prospect of public speaking, I immediately opted for the brotherhood.

Accurately suspecting that I had not given the matter much thought, the local superior told me that there was no need to rush a decision. Later, the Franciscan community identified my gifts, called them forth, and ordained me a priest. Celibacy was *not* an option in that scenario; it was a given. Innocently and in good faith, I swallowed the whole enchilada.

Never in my most outrageous fantasies of that time, not once in my wildest imagination, did I envision that one day I would marry and would devote the greater part of my life to wandering the world as a vagabond evangelist! My sole contribution to my present *Sitz-im-Leben* was to go with the flow and follow the gentle movements of the Spirit of God within me.

Today I double up with laughter whenever I realize that I have started "managing" my life once more—something we all do with astounding regularity. The illusion of control is truly pathetic, but it is also hilarious. Deciding what I most need out of life, carefully calculating my next move, and generally allowing my autonomous self to run amuck inflates my sense of self-importance and reduces the God of my incredible journey to the role of spectator on the sidelines. It is only the wisdom and perspective gleaned from an hour of silent prayer each morning that prevents me from running for CEO of the universe. As Henri Nouwen once remarked, "One of the most arduous spiritual tasks is that of giving up control and allowing the Spirit of God to lead our lives."[1]

On the other hand, *presumption* is such an insidious perversion that trust is not merely tainted but corrupted by it. In presumption, we assign to God the task of doing for us what we should be doing for ourselves.

One of the *zaddiqs* (wise old birds) of the A.A. fellowship, Father Joe Martin, uses the following illustration: Imagine a man who comes and says, "Father Martin, I want to become a great heart surgeon like Dr. Michael DeBakey. I believe that all power in heaven and on earth belongs to Jesus. So lay your hands on me and ask Jesus to infuse the knowledge and skill of DeBakey. Then I'll start my practice." Old Joe blinks in disbelief and says, "Son, go to medical school, and after you have finished your residency, specialize in coronary surgery. Then apply to a hospital, attach yourself to one of the surgical wizards for several years, and maybe in thirty years you will arrive at the premier level."

Similarly, Father Martin says, picture a guy who comes and says, "Father, I am a hopeless alcoholic. I've been drinking a quart of vodka, a gallon of Chablis, and a case of beer every day for the last twenty years. I've read a lot of the miracle stories in the Bible lately, and I know that Jesus is the master of the impossible. So pray over me and tell Jesus to set me free from bondage." And Father Martin responds, "I've got a better idea. Go to Alcoholics Anonymous, attend ninety meetings in ninety days, find yourself a sponsor, diligently work the Twelve Steps under his guidance, and read the Big Book every day. In other words, do the hard work."[2]

The most common form of presumption is the expectation that God will directly and secretly intervene in human affairs. We presume that by saying, "Lord, Lord," the cancer or bankruptcy or infidelity will disappear. We presume that God answers all prayers by assuring good outcomes, that food for the widows and orphans will fall from heaven, that the Holy One infallibly guarantees a baby's safe delivery, and that God will certainly sell our house at the desired price if we plant a statue of Saint Joseph upside down in the backyard.

The theological arguments that support an interventionary God are many and varied. Frequently people report that they have experienced a physical cure or an inner healing. And they have. "Yet," as John Shea writes, "one brutal historical fact remains—Jesus is mercilessly nailed to the cross and despite the Matthean boast, twelve legions of angels did not save him from that hour. No cop-out redemption theories that say God wanted it that way explain the lonely and unvisited death of God's Son. This side of the grave Jesus is left totally invalidated by the Lord of heaven and earth. Trust in God does not presume that God will intervene."[3]

Often trust begins on the far side of despair. When all human resources are exhausted, when the craving for reassurances is stifled, when we forgo control, when we cease trying to manipulate God and demystify Mystery, then—at our wits' end—trust happens within us, and the untainted cry, "Abba, into your hands I commend my spirit," surges from the heart.

•

ALAS, ANOTHER FORM of tainted trust is dishonesty with Jesus. Sometimes we harbor an unexpressed suspicion that he cannot handle all that goes on in our minds and hearts. We doubt that he can accept our hateful thoughts, cruel fantasies, and bizarre dreams. We wonder how he would deal with our primitive urges, our inflated illusions, and our exotic mental castles. The deep resistance to making ourselves so vulnerable, so naked, so totally unprotected is our implicit way of saying, "Jesus, I trust you, but there are limits."

By refusing to share our fantasies, worries, and joys, we limit God's lordship over our life and make clear that there are parts of us that we do not wish to submit to a divine conversation.

It seems that the Master had something more in mind when he said, "Trust in me" (John 14:1b).

9

HUMBLE CONFIDENCE

One glorious October morning, two seminarians, Attila DeBattista and Osama O'Toole, decided to help each other grow in the foundational virtue of humility. Having mutually confessed their feelings of spiritual superiority over the lowly laity, they agreed to a daily regimen of savage humiliation in order to conquer their overweening pride.

"Good morning, maggot," snarled Attila.

"Hello, worm," hissed Osama.

"Your mind is a sewer."

"Your heart is a cesspool."

"Your selfishness is an obscenity."

"Your sexual fantasies are as filthy as yourself."

"You are an unrepentant liar whose salvation is in jeopardy."

"Everyone in this seminary knows that you are a loser."

Day after day these brutal salvos continued, until finally both men fled the seminary and plunged into a life of wanton self-destruction. Gnashing their teeth over their shortcomings, they sought to escape their shame through sin. Plagued by guilt, they took refuge in wine, women, and woolgathering. Wallowing in self-hatred, they found vain compensation in dereliction and debauchery.

The more guilt and shame that we have buried within ourselves, the more compelled we feel to seek relief through sin. As we fixate on our jaded motives and soiled conscience, our self-esteem sinks, and in a pernicious leap of logic, we think that we are finally learning humility.

On the contrary, a poor self-image reveals a *lack* of humility. Feelings of insecurity, inadequacy, inferiority, and self-hatred rivet our attention on ourselves. Humble men and women do not have a *low* opinion of themselves; they have *no* opinion of themselves, because they so rarely think about themselves. The heart of humility lies in undivided attention to God, a fascination with his beauty revealed in creation, a contemplative presence to each person who speaks to us, and a "de-selfing" of our plans, projects, ambitions, and soul. Humility is manifested in an indifference to our intellectual, emotional, and physical well-being and a carefree disregard of the image we present. No longer concerned with *appearing* to be good, we can move freely in the mystery of who we really are, aware of the sovereignty of God and of our absolute insufficiency and yet moved by a spirit of radical self-acceptance without self-concern.

Humble people are without pretense, free from any sense of spiritual superiority, and liberated from the need to be associated with persons of importance. The awareness of their spiritual emptiness does not disconcert them. Neither overly sensitive to criticism nor inflated by praise, they recognize their brokenness, acknowledge their gifts, and refuse to take themselves seriously.

Am I to get depressed over the huge discrepancy between what I write and what I live? Shall I flay myself as a hypocrite because I often fail to practice what I preach? Should I spend days and weeks in self-recrimination because I am slow to forgive petty grievances even though I myself have been granted gratuitous pardon by Jesus? An illustration: At a weekend retreat in Colorado Springs with ten close friends, my "impostor"—that is, the sick, slick, and subtle impersonator of my true self—was mercilessly exposed. Led by the Spirit, my brothers told me that I was dishonest, stubborn, and prone to lies, and that self-will was running riot in my life. Did I gratefully and graciously receive their criticisms? No! Immediately I became defensive; I sulked, pouted, and returned home to brood for several weeks.

A truly humble man does not fear being exposed. I do. At that retreat, my incorrigible self-importance disallowed any challenge to my integrity. Fancying myself to be something before God, I dismissed my friends' censure as untrue, callous, and vindictive. Later, when the light of Christ dawned in my darkness, I sank to my knees and prayed with the sinful but honest tax-collector in the temple, "O God, have mercy on me, a sinner" (Luke 18:13).

The great weakness in the North American church at large, and certainly in my life, is our refusal to accept our brokenness. We hide it, evade it, gloss over it. We grab for the cosmetic kit and put on our virtuous face to make ourselves admirable to the public. Thus, we present to others a self that is spiritually together, superficially happy, and lacquered with a sense of self-deprecating humor that passes for humility. The irony is that while I do not want anyone to know that I am judgmental, lazy, vulnerable, screwed up, and afraid, for fear of losing face, the face that I fear losing is the mask of the impostor, not my own!

If there is a conspicuous absence of power and wisdom in the North American church, it has arisen because we have not come to terms with the tragic flaw in our lives: the brokenness that is proper to the human condition. Without that acknowledgment, there can be little power, for as Jesus said to the apostle Paul, "My power works at its best in your weakness" (2 Cor. 12:9).

Prior to a five-day silent retreat in Grand Coteau, Louisiana, John Colette, who guided me during this interval as my spiritual director, recommended that in the hours of prayer, I let go of the successes in my personal and professional life and stand naked before God. He used the analogy of a crab coming out of its shell, naked, unprotected, and vulnerable to predators. Frantically, the crab searches for tall grass where it can retreat to build a new shell. He said, "Brennan, you have an international reputation that may be getting in the way of your encounter with God. Emerge from the shell of your accomplishments. Drop your various identities as author, evangelist, and spiritual leader, admired by your friends and respected by your reading audience. Simply present yourself to God, clinging to nothing but your humanness."

And so the hours of prayer became a death to all past achievements and any identity not grounded in truth. Soon I discovered that, in addition to alcohol, I had developed a second addiction: ministry. The attention and recognition that come from writing and preaching, teaching and counseling, had become my latest drug of choice. Even my relationship with God was predicated on my ministerial identity. In fact, my relationship with God had become a substitute for God. Instead of praise, adoration, wonder, and thanksgiving, the focus shifted to the relationship, to where I stood with God, huffing and puffing in an effort to impress him, thrashing about trying to fix myself. Placing my security in my résumé, I always felt the need to read another book, listen to another tape, make another retreat. Whenever I heard the words, "Blessed are those who know they are broken" (Matt. 5:3), I thought, *Hell, that blessing was for publicans and prostitutes who did not have my track record of unstinting service to the Kingdom of God!* My resident inner Pharisee was clearly alive and well.

Defense mechanisms are useful ploys to warp our perception of self and protect us from rejection, loss, and emotional pain. Through the smokescreen of rationalization, projection, and insulation, we remain on the merry-go-round of denial and dishonesty. Unable to accept our brokenness, we wear a thousand masks to disguise the face of fear.

Franciscan Richard Rohr writes, "Humility and honesty are really the same thing. A humble person is simply a brutally honest person about the whole truth. You and I came along a few years ago, and we're going to be gone in a few years. The only honest response to life is a humble one."[1] Alcoholics Anonymous offers a classic definition of humility: "stark, raving honesty."

Humble people are small in their own eyes, honest about their struggles, and open to constructive criticism. Following the counsel of Jesus to take the last place, they are not shocked or offended when others put them there. They trust that they are loved, accepted, forgiven, and redeemed just as they are. Aware of their innate poverty, they throw themselves on the mercy of God with carefree abandon.

Jesus said, "Learn from me, for I am gentle and humble in heart" (Matt. 11:29). In what did the humility of Jesus consist? Low self-esteem, feelings of unworthiness, disappointment with his spiritual progress? Absurd! He was enthralled with his Father. In utter self-forgetfulness, he lived for God. The central theme in his personal life was the growing intimacy with, trust in, and love of his Abba. He lived securely in his Father's acceptance. "As the Father has loved me, so have I loved you" (John 15:9), he reassures us. Jesus' inner life was centered in God. His communion with his Abba transformed his vision of reality, enabling him to perceive divine love toward sinners and scalawags. Jesus did not live from himself or for himself but from the graciousness of the Other, who is incomprehensibly caring. He understood his Father's compassionate heart.

Why was Jesus attracted to the unattractive, why did he desire the undesirable and love those deemed unlovely by human standards? Why did he love all those losers, failures, and no-accounts? Because his Father does. "I tell you most solemnly, the son can do nothing by himself; he can do only what he sees the father doing: and whatever the father does the son does too" (John 5:19). His single-minded orientation toward his Father freed him from self-consciousness. Lost in wonder and gratefulness, he taught us the true meaning of humility.

Following Jesus, the humble in heart waste little time

in introspection, navel-gazing, looking in the mirror, and being anxious about their spiritual growth. Their self-acceptance without self-concern is anchored in the acceptance of Jesus in their struggle to be faithful. They fasten their attention on God.

An old Franciscan understood the theocentric character of genuine humility and offered this counsel:

> If you feel the call of the spirit, then be holy with all your soul, with all your heart, and with all your strength. If, however, because of human weakness, you cannot be holy, then be perfect with all your soul, with all your heart, and with all your strength.
>
> But if you cannot be perfect because of the vanity of your life, then be good with all your soul. . . . Yet, if you cannot be good because of the trickery of the Evil One, then be wise with all your soul. . . .
>
> If, in the end, you can neither be holy, nor perfect, nor good, nor wise because of the weight of your sins, then carry this weight before God and surrender your life to his divine mercy.
>
> If you do this, without bitterness, with all humility, and with a joyous spirit due to the tenderness of a God who loves the sinful and ungrateful, then you will begin to feel what it is to be wise, you will learn what it is to be good, you will slowly aspire to be perfect, and finally you will long to be holy.[2]

Steeped in the Hebrew scriptures, Jesus identified the mystical tradition of the *Anawim* (the humble remnant who compounded a sense of personal powerlessness with unfailing confidence in the love of God and total surrender to the guidance of his will) with himself ("I am gentle and humble in heart") and gave that tradition pride of place in his preaching. In his inaugural address, the Sermon on the Mount, he began, "Blessed are those who know they are poor, for the kingdom of heaven is theirs" (Matt. 5:3, NEB).

Again and again he returned to this theme: "For he who humbles himself will be exalted" (Luke 18:14); the way of humility is "the narrow gate and the hard road that leads to life, and only a few find it" (Matt. 7:14).

A careful reading of the gospel message suggests that Jesus needs nothing but our humility and confidence to work miracles in us. Jesus found the humility of the Canaanite woman so irresistible that he could not refuse what she asked. "Even the dogs eat the scraps that fall from the master's table," she said. After she humbled herself in this way, Jesus exalted her: "Woman, you have great trust. Your request is granted" (Matt. 14:28). Deeply moved by the humble confidence of the thief on the cross—"Lord, remember me when you come into your Kingdom" (Luke 23:42)—Jesus canceled the man's lifetime of sin and transmogrified the ragamuffin into the first canonized saint. No million years in purgatory, no laps in the lake of fire—"*Today* you will be with me in Paradise" (v. 43).

With the memory of his triple denial engraved on his psyche, Peter wrote from his heart: "Wrap yourselves in humility and be servants of each other, because God refuses the proud and will always favor the humble" (1 Peter 5:5–6).

The humble man is surprised by all the good that he sees around him rather than scandalized by what he cannot judge anyway. The humble woman is grateful for her successes but not disheartened by her failures. She enjoys her gifts and readily admits her mistakes. She maintains a sense of humor, whether the news from Wall Street is giddy or glum. She faces her character defects without getting discouraged. Her humble confidence in God's love and her enchantment with the *kabōd Yahweh* shape a hedge of thorns against self-absorption and free her for an unselfconscious presence to others.

JESUS COMPARED the Kingdom of God to the inexplicable bounty reaped by the man who throws seed on the land. With that simple act, the farmer's work is done. He hibernates for the winter, sleeps late, goes bowling, watches television, washes clothes, repairs the hole in the roof, and travels to Delaware, New Mexico, and Oregon to visit his three children. Whether it is night or day, whether the farmer is asleep or awake, at home or on the road, the seed he scattered sprouts and grows. He does not have a clue how it happened. The earth does it all without his help. First the shoot, then the ear, then the full grain in the ear. One sunlit morning, he has six buttermilk pancakes and four slices of Canadian bacon for breakfast, walks out the door, scratches his head at the ripened grain, and reaps his harvest (Mark 4:26–29).

That is the way it is with trust. Over the years it ripens into confidence. Based on the solid, irrefutable evidence of God's relentless faithfulness, a certainty in the trustworthiness of the tremendous Lover evolves without the least sweat and strain on our part. After the farmer casts the seed on the ground, he sleeps unperturbed, and the earth "of itself"—in the Greek text, "automatically"—brings forth fruit. The growth of trust into confidence is likewise "of itself." Just as a humble person finds it easy to say, "I don't know," so the humbly confident disciple, when asked to explain his surety in the love of God, scratches his head and says, "I can't explain it because I really don't know."

When the farmer arises in the morning, unreconciled to getting out of bed, he feels no anxiety that he has wasted time through his sleep; au contraire, he is confident that the seed has continued to grow during the night. So, too, the spiritual woman does not fret and flap over opportunities missed, does not hammer herself for not working hard enough, and does not have a panic attack wondering whether she has received grace in vain.

She lives in quiet confidence that God is working in her by day and by night. Like the farmer, she is not totally passive or presumptuous. The woman knows that she has her full measure of work to do, but she realizes that the outcome rests with God and that the decisive factor is unearned grace. Thus, she works as if everything depends on God and prays as if everything depends on her. (She learned from the Trappist monk Thomas Keating that the only way to fail in prayer is not to show up.)

The farewell discourse of Jesus in the Upper Room on the eve of his death is highly significant in the trust/confidence context. For three years the apostles had enjoyed an intimate relationship with the Master. They had witnessed the raising of Lazarus, of the son of the widow of Naim; they had listened to his original aphorisms and the edged, succulent metaphors of the camel and the eye of the needle; they had felt the blood in Jesus' preaching and the fire that burned in the beatitudes; and they had witnessed the wild tumult of the people as the Great Rabbi wandered like a vagabond evangelist through Judea and Galilee. Peter had confessed him as the Christ. Peter, James, and John had witnessed his glory on Mount Tabor. Thomas had learned that to see Jesus was to see the Father. All had learned that there were reserved spaces for them in the inner apartments of eternity. As quarrelsome and slow-witted as they were, they nevertheless trusted Jesus and had entrusted their lives to him.

With time ticking away like sand sinking in an hourglass, Jesus rose from the table and spoke his final word to his friends: "I've told you all this, so that trusting me, you will be unshakable and assured, deeply at peace. In this godless world you will continue to experience difficulties. But *have confidence,* I have overcome the world" (John 16:33, *The Message* and Douay-Rheims).

Walter Burghardt writes, "When I trust you, I wed faith and hope. I rely on you to be faithful, to be true to your promises, true to yourself. It is not quite the same as confidence. Trust, Webster's Second Unabridged tells us, 'is often instinctive, less reasoned than confidence, which is apt to suggest somewhat definite grounds of assurance.'"[3]

Has the Christ of history and the Christ of our faith-journey provided those grounds of assurance? Do we demand more signs and wonders, something more spectacular (and distracting) than what Jesus did for the Eleven when, through the gift of his Spirit, they burst out of their hiding place brimming with confidence and fearlessly proclaimed the risen Christ to the assembly of Jews?

That was spectacular indeed, but equally amazing to me is the steadfast grace that allows us to remain relentlessly faithful through the disasters and disappointments, the struggles and the heartaches of the human adventure. Our graced track record instills a modest confidence that, although we often stumble and fall, we will keep getting up; that we will not be numbered among the superficial who burn their Bibles at the first sign of trouble, or the defeated who fight long and struggle honorably for their faith but eventually yield to despair; that the grace for the next step and the courage to receive it will be given.

Happily acknowledging that everything is grace, let's pray together:

> Abba, I surrender my will and my life to you today, without reservation and with humble confidence, for you are my loving Father. Set me free from self-consciousness, from anxiety about tomorrow, and from the tyranny of the approval and disapproval of others, that I may find joy and delight simply and solely in pleasing you. May my inner freedom be a compelling sign of your presence, your peace, your power, and your love. Let your plan for my life and the lives of all your children gracefully unfold one day at a time. I love you with all my heart, and I place all my confidence in you, for you are my Abba.

10

THE CRACKED POT

A water-bearer in India had two large pots. Each hung on opposite ends of a pole that he carried across his neck. One of the pots had a crack in it, while the other was perfect. The latter always delivered a full portion of water at the end of the long walk from the stream to the master's house. The cracked pot arrived only half-full. Every day for a full two years, the water-bearer delivered only one and a half pots of water.

The perfect pot was proud of its accomplishments, because it fulfilled magnificently the purpose for which it had been made. But the poor cracked pot was ashamed of its imperfection, miserable that it was able to accomplish only half of what it had been made to do.

After the second year of what it perceived to be a bitter failure, the unhappy pot spoke to the water-bearer one day by the stream.

"I am ashamed of myself, and I want to apologize to you," the pot said.

"Why?" asked the bearer. "What are you ashamed of?"

"I have been able, for these past two years, to deliver only half my load, because this crack in my side causes water to leak out all the way back to your master's house. Because of my flaws, you have to do all this work and you don't get full value from your efforts," the pot said.

The water-bearer felt sorry for the old cracked pot, and in his compassion, he said, "As we return to the master's house, I want you to notice the beautiful flowers along the path." Indeed, as they went up the hill, the cracked pot took notice of the beautiful wildflowers on the side of the path, bright in the sun's glow, and the sight cheered it up a bit.

But at the end of the trail, it still felt bad that it had leaked out half its load, and so again it apologized to the bearer for its failure.

The bearer said to the pot, "Did you notice that there were flowers only on your side of the path, not on the other pot's side? That is because I have always known about your flaw, and I have taken advantage of it. I planted flower seeds on your side of the path, and every day, as we have walked back from the stream, you have watered them. For two years I have been able to pick these beautiful flowers to decorate my master's table. Without you being just the way you are, he would not have had this beauty to grace his house."[1]

Eager to extract a moral from this lovely story, the artist of the obvious will hasten to tell us that we are all cracked pots and that we should allow Jesus to use our flaws in order to grace his Father's table. Such trite moralizing spoils the story. Using the cracked pot to serve his didactic purpose, the moralist preens his feathers by laying another burden on us, saying, in effect, Accept your clumsy, cockeyed selves, you dimwitted dorks!

Unquestionably, a moral code is indispensable for an authentic spiritual life. We are intellectually, aesthetically, and morally ill to the extent that we lack firm rootedness in ultimate reality. We are by essence transcendent beings, and as such we cannot live fully without a solid, secure commitment to values, morals, and goals.

However, incessant and exclusive moralizing reduces the Good News to a tedious behavioral code, a rigid ethic, or an altruistic philosophy of life. Martha illustrates what we become when we focus on moralizing:

> In the course of their journey Jesus came to a village, and a woman named Martha welcomed him into her house. She had a sister called Mary, who sat down at the Lord's feet and listened to him speaking. Now Martha who was distracted with all the serving said,

> "Lord, do you not care that my sister is leaving me to do the serving all by myself? Please tell her to help me." But the Lord answered: "Martha, Martha, you worry and fret about so many things, and yet few are needed, indeed only one. It is Mary who has chosen the better part; it is not to be taken from her" [Luke 10:38–42].

Many biblical scholars have interpreted this passage to contrast the merits of the contemplative life and the active life. In juxtaposing the Martha-Mary story with the parable of the good Samaritan (which precedes it), Luke—these scholars tell us—aims to establish the pre-eminence of prayerfulness over busyness by showing Jesus exasperated with Martha. (Of course, a guilt trip looms for us either way, whether we choose Martha's course and opt for the urgent and neglect the essential.)

Consider this possibility, however: acknowledging that eisegesis[2] can be a slippery slope, we can state unequivocally that Jesus is not only the center of the gospel message but the *whole* gospel. The four evangelists never focus, in all their narratives, on another personality. Fringe women stay on the fringe; marginal men remain on the periphery. No one is allowed to take center stage. Various individuals are introduced only to interrogate, respond, or react to Jesus. Nicodemus, Peter, Thomas, Martha, Mary, Caiaphas, Pilate, and a score of others are background to the person of Jesus.

He dwarfs everyone else. This is as it should be, for the gospel is *kairos,* the hour of salvation. This is the proper theological understanding of the New Testament and the eschatological Lordship of Jesus Christ.

Martha and Mary are clearly not the focus of the Lucan narrative. So what does the passage tell us about *Jesus?* He is en route to Jerusalem, aware already of the hostile reception awaiting him. He interrupts his journey to stop at the village of Bethany. Exhausted from the hurly-burly of ministry, heavy-hearted with the intrigue of the Pharisees and the pettiness of the apostles, longing for female companionship, he seeks out his two dear friends. Intuitively understanding his need, Mary allows Jesus to pour out his heart, giving him rapt, undivided attention and affection. Martha, who is hungry, assumes that her guest is more interested in food than conversation and launches into the ministry of hospitality. She thinks that her ditsy sister should get with the program and asks Jesus to straighten her out.

Jesus' response conveys this essence: "Cool it, Martha. We'll have the trout almondine later. I'm worn out, lonely, empty, and frightened. I'm heading to the Holy City, and as you know, a prophet must die in Jerusalem. Drop the frying pan, come over here, sit beside your sister, and hold my hand. I need you. Mary's got a grip on where I'm at. She knows that I'm fully human, have a sensitive human heart, and long to be treated as a man who is human."

He might add, for our benefit, "In praying the scriptures, don't be content with the words written on the page but move through them into my presence, and—with Mary—grow still, be attentive, and listen."

The water-bearer stunned the cracked pot with the words, "Without you being just the way you are, the master would not have had this beauty to grace his house." The pot had assumed that the sole purpose of its existence was to haul water from the stream to the house. Enfolded within its narrow self-determination, the flawed pot had not suspected God's grand purpose for it: to give life to the dormant flower seeds along the path.

Does not this restricted view describe our own situation? We formulate plans to fulfill what we perceive to be the purpose of our lives (inevitably limited), and when the locomotive of our longings gets derailed, we deem ourselves failures. For example, I rented an office here in New Orleans. Why? Ostensibly to be alone and undistracted in order to write a book. For three months I found myself crippled by writer's block. With each passing day, internal pressure increased and tension mounted. One day, frustrated, I walked around the apartment complex. Eighty-year-old Johnny, unable to drive and barely able to walk, called out, "Hey, kid, can you do me a favor?"

"What?" I asked.

"Would you go to the store for me?"

Thus began the twice-a-week ritual of tripping to Sav-a-Center to fetch the staples of his diet: wieners, white bread, Coca-Cola, and a lemon or chocolate pie.

One day in prayer the Holy Spirit whispered, "The function of this office is to serve the purpose of your life: to spend time in prayer, loving God with all your heart, mind, and strength, and to go to the store for Johnny. The book is lagniappe." Then, like a bell sounding in my soul, came the words of Meister Eckhart, who insisted that the entire goal of the spiritual life is compassion. "If you were in an ecstasy as deep as that of St. Paul and there was a sick man who needed a cup of soup, it were better for you that you returned from the ecstasy and brought the cup of soup for love's sake."

Our disappointments arise from presuming to know the outcome of a particular endeavor. The cracked pot was clueless about its life-giving purpose as a vessel. Often we preachers are crestfallen when "our most 'telling' remarks fall flat," as Simon Tugwell notes, "and our most unrehearsed and immature thoughts bear fruit. People's lives are changed by casual sayings they misunderstand or mishear."[3]

The eleventh step of the Alcoholics Anonymous program is this: "Sought to improve my conscious contact with God through prayer and meditation, seeking only the knowledge of his will for us and the power to carry it out." After delivering what I considered to be a dazzling explanation of the step—an interpretation filled with profound theological, spiritual, and psychological insights, I proceeded to use an innocuous illustration:

> A monk was being pursued by a ferocious tiger. He ran as fast as he could until he reached the edge of the cliff. He noticed a rope hanging over the cliff, grabbed it and shimmied down the side of the cliff. Then the monk glanced down and saw a big, jagged rock five hundred feet below. Then the monk glanced up and saw the tiger poised over the cliff. Just then, two mice began to chew on the rope. What to do?
>
> The monk looked at the face of the cliff, saw a strawberry growing, reached out, plucked it, ate it and cried, "Yum-yum. That's the best strawberry I've ever tasted." If he had been preoccupied with the rock below, the future, or with the tiger above, the past, he would have missed the strawberry that only comes in the present moment.

Later a woman at the meeting approached me and said, "I loved your story about the strawberry." "Yuck," said I. "Ugh," said she. We nodded in clandestine agreement that one humble strawberry had more power than all my "telling" and pompous inanities. Sometimes, as Tugwell notes, our conscious intentions do little more than provide the comic interludes in the drama of our lives.

Consider the therapist who gives "telling" advice about a problem that the client does not even have. The client then concludes that the therapist is a space cadet and, in the providential design of God, finds a therapist who actually helps her. Or consider the man outraged by a murder in his neighborhood who seeks the advice of his pastor. The cleric's sage counsel so infuriates the man that he discovers what the obsession to murder feels like and comes to resolution and understanding. We are as unaware as the cracked pot of the divine intention in much of what we do. Entrusting ourselves to Mystery, we move forward fearlessly, knowing that the future of the planet probably does not depend on what we do next.

THE CRACKED POT was sad because it compared itself to the perfect pot. Without the comparison, it would have been happy, content in the knowledge that it was exactly the way it was supposed to be.

An obese woman is merry until she compares herself to Naomi Campbell. A fledging writer is at peace until he compares himself to William Faulkner. An adequate quarterback is satisfied until he compares himself to Joe Montana. I'm okay until I compare myself to Mother Teresa.

Israel Schwartz was sad because he wasn't like Moses. One night an angel appeared to him and said, "On Judgment Day, Yahweh will not ask you why you were not Moses; he will ask you why you were not his beloved Izzy."

From infancy we are taught to compare ourselves to others in terms of intelligence, talent, charisma, and physical appearance. Infants appear in television commercials, beauty pageants are held for six-year-olds, IQ tests are administered in third grade, and Little League mania rules many a home. SAT scores, class rankings, and success in the stock market—along with competitions and rivalries in every arena of life—compel us to measure our worth, for better or worse, on a scale that does not exist in the mind of God. The slightest crack is unacceptable, inducing a deadening sense of inferiority. If I cannot write with the grace, guts, and glory of Philip Yancey, I conclude in despair, I will have to settle for writing soporific slogans on greeting cards.

Jungian analyst Robert Johnson relates the story of a famous monastery in which every monk was an expert in some high art—except for one little fellow, who had no expertise in any of the celebrated gifts of his brothers. Feeling terribly inadequate, one day he decided to give to the mother of Jesus the only thing he had to offer: having been a tumbler in the circus before going to the monastery, he decided to perform for her.

> Several days later, when all the other monks were up in the chapel participating in the high mass, the little

monk went down into the crypt. He was such a nobody in the monastery that no one missed him or knew where he was. He found himself entirely alone in the crypt and began to perform his circus tumbling act before the statue of the Virgin.

This went on for some time, until one day another monk came down to the crypt to fetch candles and witnessed this strange scene. He was scandalized and immediately ran to the abbot. "Your holiness, do you know what is going on in the crypt during high mass?" The abbot had some perception, and he told the monk that they would meet the following day and go down to the crypt to witness the scene.

The next day during high mass, the abbot and the informer left the sanctuary and went down to the crypt to see what was going on. Sure enough, there was the little monk doing his tumbling act before the statue of the Virgin. The informer was by this time shaking with outrage, but the abbot held him back and continued to watch. When the tumbling was over, the Holy Virgin came down off the pedestal, held out her hand, and blessed the small monk for what he had done.

The abbot turned to the informer and said, "More real worship goes on here than takes place upstairs."

It is told that the tumbler became the next abbot of the monastery, ushering in a golden age.[4]

The apostle John writes, "A man can lay claim only to what is given him from heaven" (3:27). Any attempt to measure the value of our lives by comparison and contrast to others belittles our gifts and dishonors God by our ungratefulness. As an old black preacher on a red-clay road in Georgia instructed a pilgrim, "Be who you is, 'cause if you ain't who you is, you is who you ain't."

UNTIL THE WATER-BEARER'S revelation, the cracked pot was in a bad space. Stalked by self-consciousness and groveling in self-concern, it was distraught over its inadequacy. And so it is with us. The self-induced stress wrought by self-consciousness leads us into depression and despair. We are indignant when an emotionally impaired fan turns fanatic and stalks TV host David Letterman at his Greenwich, Connecticut, home. Yet we serve herbal tea and Tootsie Rolls to self-absorption, which stalks us day and night and even infiltrates our dreams.

The cordial welcome extended to the self-conscious psyche brings not a blessing but a curse. Narcissism creeps in, and "the ego replaces the self-forgetfulness of wonder and gratitude."[5] What Sebastian Moore calls "the inescapable narcissism of consciousness" causes not only a fascination with self but a sense of dread: beneath our inflated (or deflated) sense of self lurks the fear that we have no interior life at all. Optimistic or pessimistic possibilities of life down the line mask an inner suspicion that our relationship with God is pretense and that we are merely parroting the words and feelings of others without internal conviction. A terrifying feeling of emptiness invades our heart, and a NO EXIT sign is posted over every passage of escape. Self-consciousness has seeded self-hatred. Relating to the cracked pot, we often feel the need to apologize to the water-bearers of our life.

Merton, who struggled with low self-esteem, saw the only way out of self-consciousness as "the innocence of pure presence to the present moment."[6] Whether savoring the taste of Bananas Foster, listening to a Mozart concerto, sniffing the scent of a rose, staring at a spider's web, touching the velvet skin of a baby, paying attention to the person speaking to us, or conscientiously "wasting" time in prayer, we can find immediate release and relief from the Stalker by being in the now. Truth to tell, there is *only* now. I suspect that Thoreau's oft-quoted comment, "I do not want to die without having lived," grew out of the awareness that self-absorption and preoccupation with the yesterdays and tomorrows of life to the neglect of the present is not living at all. (More on this theme in the next chapter.)

So where are the painful reflections of this chapter leading us? What is the theme they address? It is this: trust yourself as one entrusted by God with everything you need to live life to the full.

Despite our physical cracks, intellectual limitations, emotional impairments, and spiritual fissures, we are providentially equipped to fulfill the unique purpose of our existence. By using his humble gift, the tumbler gave more pleasure to God than the entire community of more talented monks—". . . and the last shall be first." That the pot's weakness became its strength underlines the insight of St. Augustine: "All things work together for the good of those who love God, *even our sins*."[7] A key promise made by alcoholics recovering with the help of A.A. reads, "No matter how far down the scale we have gone, we will see how our experience can benefit others."

From another perspective, Robert Johnson tells of a vision in which his soul was on trial:

> A prosecutor presented all the sins of commission and omission that I was responsible for throughout my life, and the list was very long indeed. That went on for hours, and it fell on me like a landslide. I was feeling worse and worse to the point where the soles of my feet were hot. After hours of accusations from the prosecution, a group of angels appeared to conduct my defense. All they could say was, "But he loved." They began chanting this over and over in a chorus: "But he loved. But he loved. But he loved." This continued until dawn, and in the end, the angels won, and I was safe.[8]

The Word testifies that love covers a multitude of sins. Speaking of a notorious sinner, Jesus says to Simon the Pharisee, "Her many sins have been forgiven—for she loved much" (Luke 7:47, NIV). Trust Jesus, trust the love in your heart, and trust the Word just spoken to you. With all your cracks and fissures, you are capable of greatness in the new Israel of God.

However, in our faithful listening to God's Word, we often neglect his first word to us—the gift of ourselves to ourselves: our existence, our temperament, our personal history, our uniqueness, our flaws and foibles, our identity. Our very existence is one of the never-to-be-repeated ways God has chosen to express himself in space and time. Because we are made in God's image and likeness, you and I are yet another promise that he has made to the universe that he will continue to love it and care for it.

Yet even if we accept the fact that we are a word uttered by God, we may not grasp what he is trying to say through us. In *Seeds of Contemplation* Merton writes, "God utters me like a word containing a partial thought of himself. A word will never be able to comprehend the voice that utters it. But if I am true to the concept God utters in me, if I am true to the thought in him I was meant to embody, I shall be full of his actuality and find him everywhere in myself, and find myself nowhere. I shall be lost in him."[9]

In patient endurance we wait for God to make clear what he wants to say through us. Such waiting demands not only alert attention but the courage to let ourselves be spoken. Such courage arises from unfailing trust in the wisdom of God, WHO UTTERS NO FALSE WORD.

I have known Bob Krulish, a former pro basketball player, since 1984. A couple years after our first encounter I met his son, Daniel. Born with multiple learning handicaps, he endured surgeries and therapies without complaint. One day he was asked, "Dan, if you could be somebody else, who would it be?" He did not hesitate. "No one. I like myself just the way I am." On December 28, 1997, Daniel died at age twenty-three in Denver, when the Christmas tree in his apartment caught fire, sealing off the only exit.

How glorious the splendor of a human heart which trusts that it is loved! Dan Krulish ravished the heart of God. He was the cracked pot and the tumbler fused into one.

11

THE GEOGRAPHY OF NOWHERE

Amid the breathtaking beauty of County Kerry in southwestern Ireland, Fionn MacCumhaill asked his followers,

"What is the finest music in the world?"

"The cuckoo calling from the tree that is highest in the hedge," cried his merry son.

"A good sound," said Fionn. "And Oscar," he asked, "what is to your mind the finest of music?"

"The top of music is the ring of a spear on a shield," cried the stout lad.

"It is a good sound," said Fionn.

And the other champions told their delight: the belling of a stag across the water, the baying of a tuneful pack heard in the distance, the song

> of a lark, the laughter of a gleeful girl, or the whisper of a loved one.
>
> "They are good sounds all," said Fionn.
>
> "Tell us, chief," one ventured, "what do you think?"
>
> "The music of what is happening," said great Fionn, "that is the finest music in the world."[1]

The music of what *is* happening can be heard only in the present moment, right *now,* right *here.*

Now/here spells *nowhere.* To be fully present to whoever or whatever is immediately before us is to pitch a tent in the wilderness of Nowhere. It is an act of radical trust—trust that God can be encountered at no other time and in no other place than the present moment. Being fully present in the now is perhaps the premier skill of the spiritual life.

More often than not, I do not hear the music of what is happening now because my mind ricochets between the past and the future. This morning at prayer, for example, recollection of a heartwarming telephone conversation with a friend yesterday and anticipation of a lecture at New Orleans Baptist Seminary tomorrow kidnapped my attention to God. I recited a few mechanical prayers, but my mind and heart were elsewhere and otherwise. I was King Claudius in *Hamlet:* "My words fly up, my thoughts remain below; words without thoughts never to heaven go."

Thoreau's oft-quoted comment, "I went to the woods because I wished to live deliberately, to front only the essential facts of life, and see if I could learn what it had to teach, and not, when I come to die, discover that I had not lived,"[2] likely originated from the awareness that preoccupation with the yesterdays and tomorrows of life to the neglect of now/here—Nowhere—is not living at all. When my mind is replaying past glories and defeats or imagining unknown tomorrows, the music of what *is* happening is muted. When I spin fearful scenarios about the future, my agitation prohibits any awareness of the living present.

My mother-in-law once told me a story of a Cajun who was working with a hoe in his vegetable patch. A man ran up to him shouting, "Reechard, Reechard, come quick. Your house is on fire." The Cajun dropped his hoe and ran lickety-split down the road, dreading what lay ahead. Suddenly he stopped, reined in his runaway mind, and exclaimed, "What the hell am I worried about? My name ain't Reechard, and I don't own a house!" Attending to the present moment under stress indicates an unshaken sense of self-possession. As John Shea notes, it is one of the best ways to become aware that the terrors of the unknown future are born in and nurtured solely by the mind.[3]

Yet, someone may protest, "I am completely engaged in Nowhere, and it is flat, dull, empty. No music whatsoever. I am bored. Nowhere is vastly overrated." Reply: "Sir, Madam, you are *not* engaged! If you were, you would be utterly unaware that you are bored. The constricting sickness of self-consciousness has kidnapped your attention to what *is*." Self-forgetfulness is a prerequisite for truly being in the now. As Thomas Merton observed one day, "I have the honor of having a very small gold-winged moth settling in my hand, remaining with me in its delicate perfection until I blow it away." A veritable symphony in one little moth.

Is such presence to the present reserved for monks and mystics? Not at all. Marv Levy, former head coach of the Buffalo Bills, was on the field at Cleveland Stadium for a nationally televised Monday night game against the Browns. He had just been diagnosed with prostate cancer and had decided not to inform his players, so as not to distract them from the combat ahead. Levy turned to his assistant coach at one point that evening and said, "Look around you, John. What a place this is! Babe Ruth hit home runs here. Jimmy Foxx hit homers here. Think about the great football players who played here—Jim Brown and Otto Graham. Isn't it magnificent? I mean, is there any place on earth you would rather be right now than right here?"[4]

Hollywood film director John Frankenheimer was asked if he got nervous before shooting an eighty-million-dollar movie with megastars. "The most important thing for me as a human being and a movie director," he answered, "is to give undivided presence to the present. The past is something I can't do anything about. The future is terrifying because none of this ends well, as we know. So you have to stay right here, right now."[5]

To stand stubbornly in Nowhere, rejecting the restlessness that urges us to move on, silencing the voices that entice us into tomorrow, and blowing off the demonic whisper, "Look busy—Jesus is coming," is an act of unflappable trust in the presence of God, who dwells only in the unreduced immediacy of what Martin Buber called the "lived concrete."

Sue Monk Kidd quotes her mentor, Beatrice Bruteau: "Be what you are actually doing at the present moment. If you are plowing, plow fully in the moment with your whole mind and heart—in other words, 'become plowing.'" Kidd adds, "I once read an Hasidic story about a teacher who was said to have lived an unusually abundant life. After his death, one of his pupils was asked, 'What was the most important to your teacher?' The pupil replied, 'Whatever he happened to be doing at the moment.'"[6]

There is only now. Thus Jesus counsels, "Do not worry about your life, what you *will* eat or what you *will* drink or about your body, what you *will* wear" (Matt. 6:25, italics mine, NAB). Instead, Jesus says, "Look at the birds"(v. 26, NAB). After instructing us not to have a hissy fit about what may or may not happen tomorrow, he adds a bit of dark humor: "Today's trouble is enough for today" (v. 34, NRSV).

One of the fringe benefits of being Nowhere is freedom from concern about our spiritual condition. Being in the now removes us from endless and fruitless self-analysis. Moreover, in the absence of self-observation, guilt and shame mysteriously disappear. Removed from the sphere of our feelings, thoughts, and analyses, we are free to hear the music of what is happening. Lost in Nowhere, we are found in the infinity of the eternal Now.

Quite often I find myself dissatisfied with living in Nowhere. Responding to the *moment* from my Myers-Briggs space (introvert-intuitive-feeler-perceiver) and my Enneagram Four space, I ignore the gold-winged moth as insignificant and search for drama and romanticism in every experience. Preferring agony or ecstasy to the ordinary and mundane, I try to pump up each moment with gaudy significance. Aware of my demented tendency to craft every situation into a polished diamond, friends remind me that every day is not a ten.

In Luke's Gospel, Jesus heard a beautiful melody the only place it truly exists: Nowhere. "When he looked up he saw some wealthy people putting their offerings into the treasury and *he noticed* a poor widow putting in two small coins" (21:1–2, italics mine). The music created by the widow's mite entered deeply into Jesus. The present moment was not a narrow crack between yesterday's confrontation with the chief priests and scribes over tribute to Caesar and tomorrow's betrayal by Judas and the feast of Passover. The two words "he noticed" offer profound insight into the person of Jesus, highlighting his full attention to the present moment, his watchfulness, consciousness, sensitivity, perception, and unbridled appreciation for an unobtrusive old woman who tossed in her two coins and scurried away. He was deeply moved by this ragamuffin. Since the scenario was not dramatic, I would have turned away, figuring that if you've seen one bag lady, you've seen 'em all.

Digression. Of course, hellfire preachers down the ages have ignored Jesus and manipulated this scene as skillfully as a Hollywood producer to shame us with our impecunious tithes, to mortify us with our infernal stinginess, and to send us home guilt-ridden, convinced that we have out-scrooged Scrooge. Once again, we see how incessant moralizing obscures Jesus and turns Good News into Bad News. Petulant preachers inspire incredible self-harshness. We would not inflict on our dog the abuse we heap on ourselves. As Gerald May notes, "The most religious of us are so terrified of appearing selfish that we subject ourselves to unnameable and internal cruelties. And those of use who *are* more selfish stuff ourselves with poisons and whip ourselves into self-destructive highs. Some of us are meaner than others, but I have yet to meet a person in modern western culture who was not in some way cruelly self-abusive."[7] The issue of almsgiving is to be taken up with Jesus directly, not with some pantywaist preacher. *Digression concluded.*

Obdurate trust that the present moment is not merely *a* path but *the* path to communion with God has so biased Sr. Noel Toomey, my spiritual director, that she once told me flat out that my ongoing conversion would fizzle should I fail to seek God in the here and now.

Clearly, uninterrupted, sustained presence to each moment is a physical and psychological impossibility. Nor, in fact, is it desirable. Suppers would be unprepared, birthdays unobserved, World Series tickets unreserved, washers and dryers unpreserved, grades uncurved, the IRS unnerved, and meter maids unserved—and your cheese would slide completely off your cracker. Calm foresight regarding future engagements and appointments is responsible behavior, so long as it is not a compulsive escape from Nowhere.

IT IS THROUGH immersion in the ordinary—the apparently empty, trivial, and meaningless experiences of a routine day—that life/Life is encountered and lived. Real living is not about words, concepts, and abstractions but about *experience* of who or what is immediately before us. The self-forgetfulness that such experience requires is the essence of contemplative simplicity.

In his book *The Miracle of Mindfulness*, the Vietnamese Buddhist monk Thich Nhat Hanh recalls a visit from a Christian leader named Jim Forest. After the two men had dinner together, Nhat Hanh prepared to wash the dishes before serving tea and dessert, as was his custom.

> So they finished dinner and Nhat Hanh said he would wash the dishes before getting the tea. Jim offered to do the dishes, while Nhat Hahn was preparing the tea; but Nhat Hahn said, "I am not sure you know how to wash dishes." Jim laughed at him and said, "Of course I know how to wash dishes. I've been doing it all my life." "No," the monk said, "you would be washing the dishes in order to have your tea and dessert. That is not the way to wash dishes. You must wash dishes to wash dishes."[8]

Washing the dishes is not a mindless interlude before the banana cream pie. Rather, at its best—done with alertness and attention to the washing—it is excellent preparation for prayer.

As I write these pages, it is Thanksgiving Eve. I have just completed a three-mile walk at a rapid pace. As I walked this afternoon, at no time was I aware that I was walking. Images of Cajun-basted turkey, oyster and cornbread stuffing, garlic mashed potatoes, stuffed mirliton, and pecan and pumpkin pie slathered with whipped cream danced before my eyes. I was fully present to the next day.

The master once said to his pupil, "When you walk, walk; when you eat, eat." The pupil said, "But doesn't everyone do that?" "No," the master said. "Many people when they walk are interested only in getting to the place where they are going. They are not really experiencing the walking. They do not even notice that they are walking. And many people, when they eat, are more involved in making plans about what they will do after they eat. This inattention to what they are doing means that they scarcely refer to what they are eating or to the fact they are eating. They are certainly not taking joy in the fact that they are eating."

Just as attentively washing dishes is akin to prayer, so is taking joy in eating—or in writing a memo or mowing the lawn or helping the kids with homework. "Pray always," we are told, "constantly giving thanks" (1 Thess. 5:16). And what should we give thanks for? Tomorrow's turkey? No, for the sacrament of the present moment, which, as Jean-Pierre deCaussade wrote, "is always overflowing with immeasurable riches, far more than you are able to hold."[9] To live in the present moment requires profound trust that the abundant life Jesus promised is experienced only in Nowhere.

The most fascinating and delectable fruit of attention to the here and now is *compassion*. Looking unhurriedly at a flower, staring at a small child asleep, offering a nonjudgmental presence to a hurting loved one—these acts mysteriously stir gentle feelings toward ourselves and others. Through a long, loving look at the real/Real, we are, without any deliberate effort on our part, in the presence of the Compassionate One. Something of God's creative mercy [the Holy Spirit] ripples within us, and in the innocence of pure presence our debased self-image evanesces into simple and tender self-acceptance. As Merton noted, "In our human relationships we have no need to identify others with their sins and condemn them for their actions: for we are able, in them also, to see below the surface and to guess at the presence of the inner and innocent self that is the image of God."[10] After such an experience in Thailand shortly before his death, Merton wrote in his journal, "Everything is compassion; I am swimming in it."

The effort to free ourselves from concerns and the willingness to put aside fuzzy distractions involves a kind of death in order to take up the cross of the present moment. Louis Armstrong was once asked what made Frank Sinatra so special. He answered, "If you don't hear it, you ain't got ears." In other words, without active listening you cannot hear a thing; if you attend to something only superficially, you will not hear the music of what is happening.

The commitment to living out rather than escaping the gift of life is the special province of children. They find a way to sidestep time and the ravages of progress.

They operate in another zone altogether. Watch a group of children on a playground or out in the woods throwing stones at the top of a chestnut tree to dislodge the sturdiest nuts. Novelist Dom DeLillo did just that. He found that the kids would throw stones all day if necessary so that they could take the best chestnut home and soak it in salt water. Time suspended. No hurry. Totally in and with the present moment. Or watch a little girl tie the end of her jump rope to a window grille and prevail on her little brother to turn the other end. As she stands in the middle and jumps (and jumps and jumps), time as we know it does not exist for her.

Almost all children are born with a natural inclination toward contemplation—toward long, loving looks at the Real—and a tendency to moments of thoughtful silence. A simple thing may absorb children for a long time. Wiggling their toes, for example, is such an engrossing experience that it is difficult to divert their attention to something else. However, their gift starts to wither when we insist, "Hurry up; I don't have all day."

"No wonder," says Brother David Steindl-Rast, "that so many marvelous children turn into dull adults. No wonder that their wholeness is scattered and their sense of mystery lost."

The good news is that the child within can be recovered. It can happen right now, with something as simple as giving a little one a piggyback ride or walking *slowly* down the street and listening to the music of what is happening. "Unless you change and become like little children . . . " (Matt. 18:3).

CHRISTIANITY HAS DESIGNATED certain places more sacred than others, some days holier than others, and some actions more religious than others, giving the impression that contact with God happens primarily, if not exclusively, on the first day of the week in a building called church. Confining God's presence to certain predictable times and places is restrictive and leads to the unspoken assumption that the rest of the week is irreligious. As far as Jesus is concerned, though, the Sabbath was made for people, not people for the Sabbath.

James Mackey writes: "The holiday, with its special buildings and personnel, its special ritual and food, is there simply to symbolize and thus to serve the faith which is itself a *lived* conviction that all times and places . . . and all things great and small are equally close to God as his cherished gift to all of us. Thus, religion would be left intact with all its panoply intact, but the status and function of this would be properly adjusted. This was a radical faith indeed, to live out and, very likely, to die for."[11]

Whether you are hiking the Himalayas or hanging on to a subway strap in Staten Island, dunking a doughnut in Denver or sipping a Slurpy in Sausalito, the geography of Nowhere encompasses Every/where.

12

RUTHLESS TRUST

Fourteenth-century theologian and mystic John Tauler prayed for eight years that God would send him a person who would teach him the true way of perfection. One day, while at prayer, he heard a voice from within telling him to go outside to the steps of the church, and there he would meet his mentor. He obeyed without hesitation. On the church steps Tauler found a barefoot ragamuffin in rags, wounded and caked in blood.

Tauler greeted the man cordially: "Good morning, dear brother. May God give you a good day and grant you a happy life."

"Sir," replied the ragamuffin, "I do not remember ever having had a bad day."

Stunned, Tauler asked him how that was possible, since sadness and grief are part of the human condition.

The beggar explained, "You wished me a good day, and I replied that I cannot recall ever having spent a bad day. You see, whether my stomach is full or I am famished with hunger, I praise God equally; when I am rebuffed and despised, I still thank God. My trust in God's providence and his plan for my life is absolute, so there is no such thing as a bad day."

He continued, "Sir, you also wished me a happy life. I must insist that I am always happy for it would be untruthful to state otherwise. My experience of God has taught me that whatever He does must of necessity be good. Thus, everything that I receive from his loving hand or whatever He permits me to receive from the hands of others—be it prosperity or adversity, sweet or bitter—I accept with joy and see it as a sign of his favor. For many, many years now, my first resolution each morning is to attach myself to nothing but the will of God alone. I have learned that the will of God is the love of God. And by the outpouring of His grace, I have so merged my will with His that whatever He wills, I will too. Therefore, I have always been happy."[1]

The beggar's witness to Jesus Christ lay in ruthless trust in the love of God and in the determination "for all things, give thanks" (Ithess 5:18). Later in his life, Tauler wrote that this amalgam of trust and gratitude is the shortest path to God.

So why would I refer to "*ruthless* trust"? Webster's dictionary defines the adjective *ruthless* as "without pity." I use the word, in this context of trust, to mean "without *self*-pity," because self-pity is the arch-enemy of trust.

That does not mean that *all* self-pity has to go. When the shadow of Jesus' cross darkens our space, when pain and suffering intrude and our secure, well-regulated lives are blown apart, when tragedy makes its unwelcome appearance and we are deaf to everything but the shriek of our own heartache, when courage flies out the window and the world around us suddenly seems dark and menacing, self-pity is the first, normal, unavoidable, and probably right reaction; and we only exhaust ourselves further if we attempt to suppress it. Human experience has taught me that there is no effective way to fight self-pity. Sure, we can spiritualize heartbreak, camouflage our emotions, and tap-dance into religiosity. But such bravado is a denial of our humanity, and furthermore it does not work. We are not spiritual robots but sensitive persons.

However, there comes a time when self-pity becomes malignant, seducing us into self-destructive behavioral patterns of withdrawal, isolation, drinking, drugging, and so forth. We simply ask for the grace to set a time limit on our self-pity.

The *New York Times* best-seller *Tuesdays with Morrie* is the story of a man's love for his mentor. Morrie Schwartz, a Brandeis University sociology professor, was dying of ALCS (Lou Gehrig's disease). A former student, Mitch Albom, flew from Detroit to Boston every Tuesday to spend the day with his beloved old teacher. One day Mitch asked Morrie if he ever felt sorry for himself.

> "Sometimes, in the mornings," he said. "That's when I mourn. I feel around my body, I move my fingers and my hands—whatever I can still move—and I mourn what I have lost. I mourn the slow, insidious way in which I'm dying. But then I stop mourning."
>
> Just like that?
>
> "I give myself a good cry if I need it. But then I concentrate on all the good things still in my life. On the people who are coming to see me. On the stories I'm going to hear. On you—if it's Tuesday. Because we're Tuesday people."
>
> I grinned. Tuesday people.
>
> "Mitch, I don't allow myself any more self-pity than that. A little each morning, a few tears, and that's all."[2]

The way of ruthless trust is not an abstraction but a concrete, visible, and formidable reality. It gives definition to our lives, reveals what is life-giving within us, shapes the decisions we make and the words we speak, prods our consciousness, nurtures our spirit, impacts our interaction with others, sustains our will-to-meaning in life, and gives flesh and bone to our way of being in the world.

Faith in the person of Jesus and hope in his promise means that his voice, echoing and alive in the Gospels, has supreme and sovereign authority over our lives. Ignoring the linguists and historians who keep busy "fly specking the texts for historical authenticity,"[3] as John Kirvan says, and the sophisticated exegetes of the Jesus Seminar, who are still *voting,* for God's sake, on what Jesus actually said and did not say, we take the words and sayings of the Master just as Francis of Assisi did—*literally.* And this innovative approach to Jesus' message carries radical implications for the lifestyle of a trusting disciple.

Think about it. In a world of rapid change and turbo-charged global capitalism, competition drives not only the marketplace but Christian music and book publishing, political institutions, personal relationships, museums, Hollywood, rap stars, rivalries between churches, and the very fabric of life itself. One-upmanship, social climbing, power plays, sniping and stabbing, self-aggrandizement, and so forth are the precious stones in our altar of achievement.

By contrast, in what has become his most quoted parable, Jesus raises the question, "What do you think?

Which of the three became a neighbor to the man attacked by robbers?"

"The one who treated him kindly," the religion scholar responds.

Jesus says, "Go and do the same" (Luke 10:36–37).

Commenting on the story of the good Samaritan, Thomas Cahill writes, "As we stand now at the entrance to the third millennium since Jesus, we can look back over the horrors of Christian history, never doubting for an instant that if Christians had put kindness ahead of devotion to good order, theological correctness, and our own justifications—if we had followed in the humble footsteps of the heretical Samaritan who was willing to wash someone else's wounds, rather than in the self-regarding steps of the priest and the immaculate steps of the Levite—the world we inhabit would be a very different one."[4]

In Matthew, Jesus—the Way, the Truth, and the Life—says, "I tell you solemnly, insofar as you did this to one of the least of these brothers of mine, *you did it to me*" (25:40, italics mine). Placing absolute trust in this living Word, St. Cuthbert, having just received a beautiful horse from the king because the former is limp and aging, rides down the road, sees a ragged beggar, and gives him the horse. Word reaches the king. He is angry. At their next meeting the king says to Cuthbert, "I gave you a magnificent horse and you squandered it on a worthless beggar. I should have given you a sorry old mare."

"Ah, my beloved king," says Cuthbert, "you value the son of a thoroughbred more than you value a son of God."[5]

I spent Christmas Eve in the Bowery of New York City in 1970. During the day I worked with a Catholic Worker team that tended to the hungry and homeless. After helping serve an evening meal to perhaps eighty or ninety street people, I was invited upstairs to visit with Dorothy Day, the seventy-three-year-old founder of the Catholic Worker Movement. Crocheting in a battered old rocker, she welcomed me warmly and said, "Brennan, I'm sure that you are familiar with Peter Claver."

"Yes, ma'am," I replied. "Back around the 1640s he had a ministry to blacks who had been commandeered into the slave trade, often beaten to a pulp and left for dead. Claver burned out his short life, like a modern-day paramedic, alleviating their suffering or providing them care and spiritual comfort when they died."

This wizened old woman who cried the gospel with her life said, "One night Peter recruited a couple of volunteers to help minister to a dying man whose suppurating flesh had been eaten away because of years in chains. When the volunteers saw the oozing flesh and smelled the putrid odor, they ran panic-stricken from the room. Peter cried out, 'You mustn't go. You can't leave him—it is Christ.'"

Dorothy nodded, indicating that our visit was over, and asked my blessing. I kissed her hand and then, shaking in my shoes, walked out the door.

Our culture says that ruthless competition is the key to success. Jesus says that ruthless compassion is the purpose of our journey.

"THE WORD was made flesh and pitched his tent among us" (John 1:14). Mind spinning, legs wobbling, joints trembling, one kneels before a squirming baby lying in a feeding trough for cattle and whispers with doubting Thomas, "My Lord and my God" (John 20:28). Jesus is my Savior. Incarnation—living proof that infinite Love does such things. The world of theories left behind. Only silent wonder and adoration. "He emptied himself . . . " (Phil. 2:7). Omnipotence wrapped in the bonds of my own fragile humanity. The enormity of this gift calls for a response of ruthless trust.

Ruthless trust is Teresa of Avila persevering in prayer for eighteen years without one comforting emotion, believing "that God will see justice done to his chosen who cry out to him day and night even when he delays to help them" (Luke 18:7). Ruthless trust is heeding the admonition "not to parade your good deeds before men to attract their notice . . . " (Mat. 6:1) and instead routinely performing hidden, secret acts of kindness that no one will ever know about, confident that "your Father who sees all that is done in secret will reward you" (Matt. 6:6). Ruthless trust is hanging tough in the dark nights, when we are plunged into desolation but know that the absence of God is only *apparent*. As Bede Griffiths said, "I feel myself in the void, but the Void is totally saturated with love."

"If we say we have no sin in us, we are deceiving ourselves and refusing to admit the truth" (1 John 1:8). We live in a society that luxuriates in the therapeutic and the exculpatory, condemns judgment as authoritarian, dismisses acknowledgment of sin as an assault on self-worth, and resists discernment of spirits as the imposition of arbitrary standards. The devastating consequence of these societal shortcomings is the perennial gnostic retreat from personal responsibility.

If we avoid any confrontation with authentic guilt, we stifle personal growth. If we continue to blame others for our weaknesses and failures, we refuse accountability for the present direction of our life. Although self-pity thwarts self-acceptance, wearing the scarlet letter V (for victim) allows us to take the moral high ground.

My psychiatrist friend Bob Stewart once told me of a patient, a married woman whose seven-year affair with a married man had ended abruptly when he dumped her for a younger woman. Unable to face her essential unhappiness, she had blamed her loveless marriage for her infidelity and had sought therapy and pills in order to exonerate herself from her self-inflicted suffering. Finally, severely depressed and suicidal, unresponsive to antidepressant medication, she was hospitalized.

Because this woman did not hold herself morally responsible, she disdained any sense of personal guilt. For the same reason, she turned to a psychiatrist for relief rather than to the Jesus of her childhood. In a world where the only plea is "not guilty," what possibility is there of an honest encounter with Jesus, "who died for our sins"? We can only *pretend* that we are sinners, and thus only *pretend* that we are forgiven.

To knife through our pretense, cowardice, and evasions, to see the truth about ourselves and the true state of our souls before God—this requires enormous courage and ruthless trust in the merciful love of the redeeming God. Put simply, sin must be acknowledged and confessed before there can be forgiveness and real transformation.

If the readers of this book knew my whole life-story, knew how often I have wandered into the far country, knew of the lapses and relapses, the pettiness, the self-absorption, the insatiable appetite for approval, the laziness, and the exotic castles in Spain I'm always building, they would blush. I keep falling down again and again and getting up again and again, trusting that when Jesus responded to Peter's question about how often he should forgive his brother—the response was "No, not seven times but seventy times seven" (Matt. 18:22)—the Master was describing *his own practice.* "Is it possible," Clinical psychologist Jim Finley asks, "that each time we stumble, fall, and rise again, God can barely bear the bliss of it?"[6]

That's assuming our intentions are good. While we all are recidivists, those who have no intention of repenting and striking out in a new direction deceive themselves and mock God's mercy.

RUTHLESS TRUST is the shriveled old man in the convalescent home who kneels down beside his bed, risking again the "null"—the felt absence of God, the hell of no-feeling that overcame him eighteen years ago when his wife and three children died in a car accident—tears of gratitude streaming down his face.

Ruthless trust is Graham Greene's whisky priest, Georges Bernanos's cure, Shusako Endo's missionary, and Brian Moore's Père.[7] Ruthless trust is the blind, penniless poet described by John O'Riordan in *The Music of What Happens.* He has no dole, no insurance, and no security. He does not know where his next meal is going to come from or where he will lay his head when night falls. And what is he doing? Composing a song of thanksgiving for the blessings of God which lift his spirit—a full measure of hope and love, a clear conscience, and a light heart. Freed from the pursuit of material things and gifted with a profound confidence in God's love, he embodies what spiritual writer Brendan Kenneally calls "an exultant spirituality"—a perspective that emerged in Ireland in days of yore. He travels light and celebrates the unfolding journey with thanksgiving.[8]

Ruthless trust is Mrs. Neylon coming to school and greeting the children with "A grand, fine morning, thanks be to God." That made good sense when the summer sun was shining through the window. But this stalwart woman, also profiled by O'Riordan, would arrive equally cheerful in the heart of winter with the rain lashing across Sliabh Luachra and her coat and her shoes all wet; and she would take the wet cap off her head and shake it, saying, "A grand, wet morning, thanks be to God." What lay in her heart was relentless trust that every morning was *God's* morning. Hail, rain, or snow—it was the gift of God, and the only appropriate response was thanksgiving.[9]

(I cannot help but think of the many times I have lamented, "Oh, poor me," when my golf game has been rained out. If self-pity were blacktop, I could pave a road from the West Bank of New Orleans to the tip of Bora Bora.)

Ruthless trust is the spirit of those disciples of Christ who refuse to substitute the rhetoric of ideals for personal commitment.

Now let me speak to an entirely different cadre of Christians—the company of beleaguered believers who are racked with uncertainty, tormented by doubts, and haunted by unanswered questions. They are sold out to Christ, and yet they struggle constantly, fearing that human freedom is fatal. As one woman told me, "People say that God won't force himself on us. Well, I don't need that kind of courtesy." These individuals want to embrace the gospel, yet they cannot seem to get inside it. The most frustrating words they hear are, "You just have to *believe,*" because belief does not come easily—and sometimes not at all. Admirably, they refuse to fake it, even though that stance may mean resigning themselves to being outsiders in the faith community. But they are not outsiders in the fellowship of ragamuffins. One of the great Christian writers of our generation belongs to their company, and I consider him a spiritual giant.

These brave souls enter deeply into the existential loneliness of the human condition and refuse to quit. Where can they go to meet with their elusive deity? "I can't pray, 'Abba, I belong to you,'" a friend told me, "because it feels phony—as if I'm just mouthing words I don't really believe." Yet the mysterious love of God is fierce enough to penetrate even those who think that they cannot receive it. As they sink into the silence of infinite Mercy, the outsiders become aware of the Presence and hear a gentle voice whisper, "I am here. Do not be afraid. Within the dissonance and *contretemps* of your troubled world, I live and reign." Just as for many alcoholics, recovery begins on the far side of despair, so for the outsiders, trust lies on the far side of hopelessness. This is the experience described by the great Jewish philosopher Martin Buber, who confessed, "I am truly no *zaddik*, no one assured in God, rather a man endangered before God, a man wrestling ever anew for God's light, ever anew engulfed in God's abysses."[10]

Buber gave us this portrait of himself when he was forty years old, and it probably continued to reflect his essence for the almost half-century that he had yet to live. It comes as no surprise that the "outsiders" are uniquely called and uniquely graced to withstand the thousand-fold questions of beleaguered believers and give answer to their trembling hearts. And they are utterly credible because they have been through the same hell themselves. More than most, they understand the way of ruthless trust. Yet I can think of no one who would boast about belonging to their number.

IN THE HIGH-PROFILE Christian ministries—that is, the ministries of famous preachers, teachers, scholars, pastors, and writers, along with celebrated artists, singers, songwriters, musicians, poets, and the like—ruthless trust is shunning prestige, honor, power, fame, and the seductions of celebrity. It is a spirited rejection of what is described in the First Letter of John: "Carnal allurements, enticements for the eye, the life of empty show—all these are from the world" (2:16).

After gospel song writer and recording artist Michael Card finished a concert in Wembley Stadium in London, the audience rose to their feet in sustained, thunderous applause. Their unharnessed enthusiasm demanded one curtain call after another. When the brouhaha finally ended, Michael ran to his dressing room and called me long-distance here in New Orleans. "Please pray for me right now, Brennan," he begged. He knew that, like me, he could easily be seduced by the siren call of success, the unbounded adulation of his fans. "I don't want this stuff," he fairly shouted. "Ask Jesus to set me free." But Mike, who reminds me more of Francis of Assisi than anyone I have ever met, was free before he asked.

Ruthless trust is unhalting acceptance of the truth contained in the Irish proverb, "Bidden or unbidden, he is present."

As we enter the third millennium, ruthless trust is the courageous confidence that despite suffering and evil, terrorism and domestic conflict, God's plan in Jesus Christ cannot fail. The ensuing years will bring slow but steady progress in Kingdom values, and the day will dawn when the lion will lie down with the lamb; the East will learn the language of the West (and vice versa); blacks, whites, Asians, and Hispanics will truly communicate; our cities of garbage, apathy, and despair will experience the sunshine of a better life; and all men and women will rejoice in the Spirit that makes us one in Christ the Lord.

We are neither boozy dreamers, hopeless idealists, nor cockeyed optimists. We are not playing "the religion game." As I wrote on the first page of the first chapter, the act of trust is a ruthless act. Search your heart for the Isaac in your life—name it and then place it on the altar as an offering to the Lord—and you will know the meaning of Abrahamic trust.

"ABBA, EVERYTHING IS POSSIBLE for you. Take this cup away from me. But let it be as you, not I, would have it" (Mark 14:36). Jesus' death on Calvary is his greatest act of trust in his Father. Jesus plunges into the darkness of death, not knowing what lies on the other side, confident only that somehow his Abba will vindicate him. Jesus' voluntary disengagement from life is his supreme expression of persevering trust, and it wins for him and every one of us fullness of life. And his blessed, obstinate, importunate trust ravishes the heart of his Abba.

To be like Christ is to be a Christian.

Clearly, growth in trust cannot be self-initiated. The one thing most needed cannot be self-supplied. But there is one abundant source of trust to which we must return again and again. It flows from the barren rock of Golgotha at the feet of the crucified Christ. Contemplate the incomparable love of Jesus as he suffocates to death. "There is no greater love than this . . . " (John 15:13). For a few minutes stay face to face with the dying Jesus and hear him whisper, "I'm dying . . . to be with you."

The same love yesterday on Calvary, today in our hearts, and forever in heaven. Jesus crucified is not merely a heroic example to the church. He is the *power and wisdom of God,* his love capable of transforming our cowardly, distrustful hearts into hearts strong in the trust that they are loved. We do not have to do anything, except let our unworthy, ungrateful selves be loved *as we are.* Trust *happens!* You will trust him to the degree that you know you are loved by him.

"I am the resurrection. If anyone believes in me, even though he or she dies will live, and whoever lives and believes in me will never die. Do you believe this?" (John 11:26).

Ruthless trust ultimately comes down to this: faith in the person of Jesus and hope in his promise. In spite of all disconcerting appearances, we stare down death without nervousness and anticipate resurrection solely because Jesus has said, *"You have my word on it."*

It doesn't get any more ruthless. Either we believe in the resurrection and therefore trust in Jesus of Nazareth and the gospel he preached, or we do not believe in the resurrection and therefore do not trust in Jesus of Nazareth and the gospel he preached. If Easter is not history, we must become cynics. In other words, either we trust in the person and promise of Jesus and commit our lives to both, or we do not.

In the century just gone by, was there a bolder witness than that of Dietrich Bonhoeffer? On April 9, 1945, in a concentration camp in Flossenburg, Germany, having been condemned to death for conspiring in a plot to assassinate Adolf Hitler, Bonhoeffer broke loose from his two Nazi guards and went running toward the gallows, shouting, "O death, you are the supreme festival on the road to Christian freedom!"[11]

AH! THIS IS NOT a sigh of relief that the book is nearly done but an acronym for *at home*. Home is where the heart is. Home is a place of welcoming love, nonjudgmental acceptance, kisses, and hospitality—elements that induce a profound sense of belonging.

"Make your home in me, as I make mine in you" (John 15:4).

"If anyone loves me he will keep my word, and my Father will love him, and we shall come to him and make our home with him" (John 14:23).

"You realize, don't you, that you are the temple of God, and God himself is present in you?" (1 Cor. 3:16).

"Your body, you know, is a sacred place, the place of the Holy Spirit" (1 Cor. 6:19).

The stupendous mystery of the indwelling triune God! Ruthless trust is choosing to be a *homebody*. As you exhale breath throughout the day, let AH be a simple reminder of your true domicile. My gracious Lord has shown me that the best way to strip fear of its awesome power is to be a homebody, to stay home in the palace of Nowhere.

RUTHLESS TRUST is an unerring sense, way deep down, that beneath the surface agitation, boredom, and insecurity of life, it's gonna be all right. Ill winds may blow, more character defects may surface, sickness may visit, and friends will surely die; but a stubborn, irrefutable certainty persists that God is with us and loves us in our struggle to be faithful. A nonrational, absolutely true intuition perdures that there is something unfathomably big in the universe *(kabōd)*, something that points to Someone who is filled with peace and power, love and undreamed of creativity—Someone who inevitably will reconcile all things in himself.

RETURNING TO the central theme of this book, as stated in Chapter 1: the splendor of a human heart which trusts that it is loved gives God more pleasure and delight than Westminster Cathedral, the Sistine Chapel, and all the other human glories combined. Why does our trust offer such immense pleasure to God? Because trust is the preeminent expression of love. Thus, it may mean more to Jesus when we say, "I trust you," than when we say, "I love you."

Where am I in all this? With you, clasping hands each morning and crying out in unison, "Lord Jesus, I trust you; help my lack of trust."

NOTES

CHAPTER 1

1. Paul de Jaegher, *The Virtue of Trust* (New York: Kennedy & Sons, 1932), 12.
2. John Kavanaugh, *America* 173, no. 3 (July 29, 1995): 38.
3. Marcus J. Borg, *Jesus: A New Vision* (San Francisco: Harper & Row, 1987), 111.
4. Daniel Berrigan, *Isaiah: Spirit of Courage, Gift of Tears* (Minneapolis: Fortress Press, 1996), 37.
5. Henri Nouwen, *America* 180, no. 13 (Apr. 17, 1999): 34.
6. Daniel Considine, *Confidence in God* (Union City, NJ: Passionist Missionaries, 1938), 17.
7. Gerald May, *Simply Sane* (New York: Crossroad, 1993), 155.
8. Henri Nouwen, *The Inner Voice of Love* (New York: Doubleday, 1996), 101, 5, 12, 113.

CHAPTER 2

1. George Gallup Jr., *The Saints Among Us*. Quoted in an interview in *America* (Oct. 26, 1996): 20.
2. Henri Nouwen, *Bread for the Journey* (San Francisco: HarperSanFrancisco, 1997).
3. John Kavanaugh, *America* 73, no. 10 (Oct. 7, 1995), 24.

4. David Steindl-Rast, *Gratefulness: The Heart of Prayer* (New York: Paulist Press/Ramsey, 1984), 204.
5. *Letters of St. Ignatius Loyola* (Chicago: Loyola Univ. Press, 1959), 55. Quoted in Peter van Breeman, *Let All God's Glory Through* (New York: Paulist Press, 1992).

CHAPTER 3

1. Anne Donovan, *America* (1997). *America* is an exceptional periodical treating theology, spirituality, the arts, and the state of the worldwide church.
2. Louis Dupré, *Religious Mystery and Rational Reflection* (Grand Rapids, MI: Eerdmans, 1998), 41.
3. Dupré, *Religious Mystery and Rational Reflection*, 42.
4. Frederick Buechner, *Listening to Your Life* (San Francisco: HarperSanFrancisco, 1992), 285.
5. Raymond Nogar, *The Lord of the Absurd* (New York: Herder & Herder, 1966), 126.
6. Donovan, "Article Title," XX.
7. Philip Yancey, *What's So Amazing About Grace?* (Grand Rapids: Zondervan, 1997), 52, 70.
8. Paul R. Messbarger, *America* (1997), 37.
9. Irenaeus, *Against the Heresy of Gnosticism*.

CHAPTER 4

1. Peter van Breeman, *Let All God's Glory Through* (New York: Paulist Press, 1992), 105.
2. *USA Today* editorial, June 4, 1998:14.
3. John L. McKenzie, *Dictionary of the Bible* (New York: Macmillan, 1965), 136. This book is a stunning achievement by a single biblical scholar, with over two thousand articles covering every book of the Bible, as well as its major themes, concepts, and characters. My development of *kabōd* relies on his scholarship.

4. Quoted by John Kirvan, *God-Hunger* (Notre Dame, IN: Sorin Books, 1999), 50.
5. Fridolin Stier, *Vielleicht ist ingenduo Tag Aufzeichnungen* (Freiburg-Heidelberg: Kerle-Verlag, 1981), 205f. Quoted in van Breeman, *Let All God's Glory Through.*
6. William Johnston, *Letters to Contemplatives* (Maryknoll, NY: Orbis Books, 1991), 6.
7. Quoted in Peter van Breeman, *Let All God's Glory Through* (New York: Paulist Press, 1992).
8. Mark Altrogge, "I Stand in Awe." Published by People of Destiny Music, Pleasant Hill Music, admisistered by Word Music, 1997.
9. Thomas Aquinas, *Summa Theologica.*
10. Maurice Friedman, *Early Years* (New York: Dutton, 1982). Quoted in Friedman's *Encounter on the Narrow Ridge* (New York: Paragon House, 1993), 16.
11. Friedman, *Early Years,* 17.
12. Bernard McGinn, *The Foundations of Mysticism,* vol. 1 (New York: Crossroad, 1991), 286.
13. Trappist monk from Holland.
14. Chaim Potok, *The Book of Lights* (New York: Fawcett Crest, 1982), 104.

Chapter 5

1. Fyodor Dostoevsky, *Crime and Punishment* (New York: Bantam Classics, 1981 [1866]), 20.
2. Leo Tolstoy, *War and Peace* (Oxford: Oxford Univ. Press, 1922 [1869]), 238.
3. Karl Rahner, *Prayers for a Lifetime* (New York: Crossroad, 1995), 138.
4. Rahner, *Prayers for a Lifetime,* 138.
5. Philip Roth, *American Pastoral* (New York: Random House/ Vintage, 1998), 35.

CHAPTER 6

1. Parker Palmer, *The Monastic Renewal of the Church*. Reprinted in *The Desert Call* (periodical date, volume, and page numbers unavailable).
2. Simon Tugwell, *The Beatitudes: Soundings in Christian Tradition* (Springfield, IL: Templegate, 1980), 18.
3. James T. Burtchaell, *Philemon's Problem* (Chicago: ACTA Foundation, 1973), 18.
4. Tugwell, *The Beatitudes*, 44.
5. Godfrey Diekmann, *Come, Let Us Worship* (Baltimore: Helicon Press, 1961).
6. These observations can be verified in the writings of theologians and liturgical scholars such as Godfrey Diekmann, Yves Congar, Karl Adam, Cyprian Vaggagini, Louis Buoyer, and others.

CHAPTER 7

1. John L. McKenzie, *Dictionary of the Bible* (New York: Macmillan, 1965), 269.
2. Edward Schillebeeckx, *Interim Report on the Books Jesus and Christ* (New York: Crossroad, 1985), 52.
3. Albert Nolan, *Jesus Before Christianity* (Maryknoll, NY: Orbis Books, 1976), 137.
4. John L. McKenzie, *The Power and the Wisdom* (Milwaukee, WI: Bruce Publishing, 1965), 1550.
5. St. Augustine, *The Confessions of St. Augustine* (New York: E.P. Dutton, 1932), vol. 3, part 6, 11.
6. Bernard Lonergan, *Insight* (London: Dartman, Longman and Todd, 1957), 38.
7. Karl Rahner, *Prayers for a Lifetime* (New York: Crossroad, 1995), 39.
8. Søren Kierkegaard, *Purity of Heart Is to Will One Thing* (New York: Harper and Row, 1948), 102.
9. Michael Downey, *Hope Begins Where Hope Begins* (Maryknoll, NY: Orbis Books, 1998), 106–7.

10. Walter Burghardt, *Tell the Next Generation* (New York: Paulist Press, 1984), 42.
11. Frederick Buechner, *Brendan* (San Francisco: Harper & Row, 1988), 217.
12. Brennan Manning, *Abba's Child* (Colorado Springs, CO: 1994), 163–64. For the original, "I hate okra," I have substituted, "I hate hard rock" because the deafening, over-stimulating, soulless, maddening, pathological beat of hard rock evokes more venom than the pallid taste of okra.
13. St. Augustine, *The Confessions of St. Augustine*, 14.
14. Paul Tillich, *The Shaking of the Foundations* (New York: Charles Scribner's Sons, 1948), 42.
15. Walter Kasper, *Jesus the Christ* (New York: Paulist Press, 1977), 86.
16. Simon Tugwell, *The Beatitudes: Soundings in Christian Tradition* (Springfield, IL: Templegate, 1980), 79.
17. Thomas Merton, *The Asian Journal of Thomas Merton* (Copyright by the Merton Legacy Trust, 1973), 54.
18. Julian of Norwich (New York: Paulist Press, 1980), 196.
19. Dallas Willard, *The Divine Conspiracy* (San Francisco: HarperSanFrancisco, 1998), 13.

Chapter 8

1. Henri Nouwen, *Here and Now* (New York: Crossroad, 1994), 54.
2. Father Joe Martin, *Chalk Talk*, a series of videotapes circulating in the A.A. Fellowship for the last thirty years.
3. John Shea, *The Challenge of Jesus* (Chicago: Thomas More Press, 1975), 133–34.

Chapter 9

1. Richard Rohr, *Everything Belongs* (New York: Crossroad, 1999), 103.
2. Quoted in Peter van Breeman, *Let All God's Glory Through* (New York: Paulist Press, 1992), 134.

3. Walter J. Burghardt, *Tell the Next Generation* (New York: Paulist Press, 1980), 41.

Chapter 10

1. A story from India. Author unknown.
2. Eisegesis is imposing on a biblical text a meaning that may not be there, depending on the whim or inspired insight of the individual. Aberrations such as the frivolous attempt to match symbols from the Book of Revelation with historical events today in order to prophesy the imminent end of the world are current examples of eisegesis. Exegesis, on the other hand, is drawing from the text itself the explanation or critical interpretation.
3. Simon Tugwell, *The Beatitudes: Soundings in Christian Tradition* (Springfield, IL: Templegate, 1980), 38.
4. Robert A. Johnson and Jerry Michael Ruhl, *Balancing Heaven and Earth* (San Francisco: HarperSanFrancisco, 1998), 284–85.
5. Suzanne Zuercher, *Merton: An Enneagram Profile* (Notre Dame, IN: Ave Maria Press, 1996), 92.
6. Zuercher, *Merton: An Enneagram Profile*, 92.
7. St. Augustine, *The Confessions of St. Augustine*, 212.
8. Johnson and Ruhl, *Balancing Heaven and Earth*, 173–74.
9. Thomas Merton, *Seeds of Contemplation*.

Chapter 11

1. John J. O'Riordan, *The Music of What Happens* (Winona, MN: St. Mary's Press, 1997), 109–10.
2. Henry D. Thoreau, *Walden* (New York: Dodd, Mead and Co., 1946), xi.
3. John Shea, *Starlight* (New York: Crossroad, 1993), 117.
4. *Sports Illustrated*, Nov. 27, 1995: 41.
5. *Newsweek*, April 27, 1998: 60.

6. Sue Monk Kidd, *When the Heart Waits* (San Francisco: HarperSanFrancisco, 1990), 193–94.
7. Gerald May, *Simply Sane* (New York: Crossroad, 1997), 164.
8. Thich Nhat Hanh, *The Miracle of Mindfulness*. Quoted by William H. Shannon, *Silence on Fire* (New York: Crossroad, 1991), 74.
9. Jean-Pierre deCaussade, *The Sacrament of the Present Moment* (San Francisco: HarperSanFrancisco, 1989), 53.
10. Suzanne Zuercher, *Merton: An Enneagram Profile* (Notre Dame, IN: Ave Maria Press, 1996), 143.
11. James Mackey, *Jesus: The Man and the Myth* (New York: Paulist Press, 1979), 171.

Chapter 12

1. George Maloney, *In Jesus We Trust* (Notre Dame, IN: Ave Maria Press, 1990), 129.
2. Mitch Albom, *Tuesdays with Morrie* (New York: Doubleday, 1997), 56–57.
3. John Kirvan, *God Hunger* (Notre Dame, IN: Sorin Books, 1999), 14.
4. Thomas Cahill, *Desire of the Everlasting Hills* (New York: Doubleday, 1999), 185.
5. O'Riordan, *The Music of What Happens*, 156.
6. James Finley, *The Contemplative Heart* (Notre Dame, IN: Sorin Books, 2000), 57.
7. Graham Greene, *The Power and the Glory* (New York: Penguin Books, 1995); Georges Bernanos, *The Diary of a Country Priest* (New York: Carroll & Graf, 1984); Shusako Endo, *A Life of Jesus*, trans. Richard Schuchert (New Jersey: Paulist Press, 1989); Brian Moore, *Blackrobe—A Novel* (New York: Plume, 1997).
8. John J. O'Riordan, *The Music of What Happens* (Winona, MN: St. Mary's Press, 1997), 69.

9. O'Riordan, *The Music of What Happens*, 70.
10. Maurice Friedman, *Encounter on the Narrow Ridge* (New York: Paragon House, 1993), 53–54.
11. Geffrey B. Kelly, *Liberating Faith* (Minneapolis: Augsburg Pubulishing House, 1984), 31.